Piano • Vocal • Guitar

The Three Chord Songbook

ISBN 978-1-5400-0568-7

HAL•LEONARD®

7777 W. BLUEMOUND RD. P.O. BOX 13819 MILWAUKEE, WI 53213

Visit Hal Leonard Online at
www.halleonard.com

Contents

ALL ABOUT THAT BASS

Words and Music by KEVIN KADISH
and MEGHAN TRAINOR

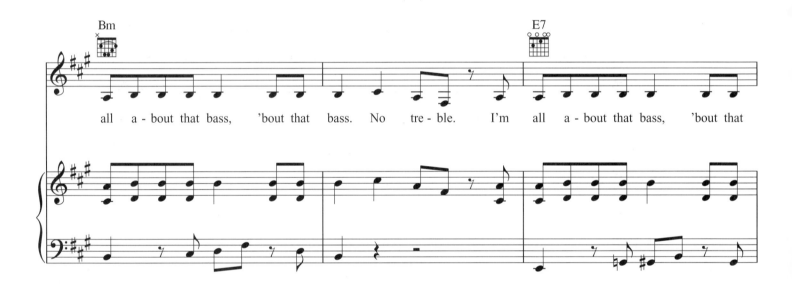

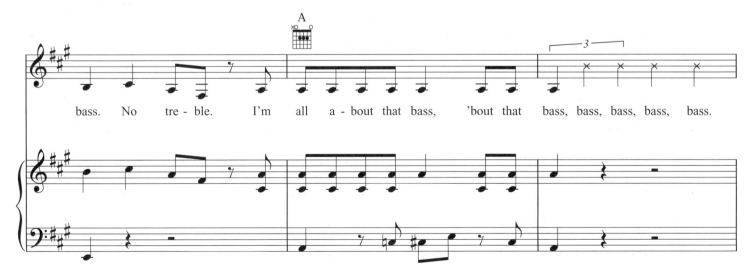

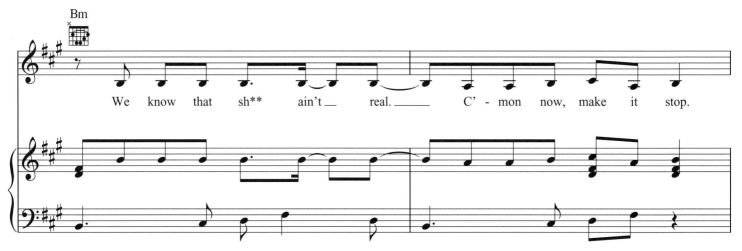

We know that sh** ain't __ real.___ C' - mon now, make it stop.

If you got beau - ty, beau - ty, just raise 'em up 'cause ev - 'ry inch of you is per - fect from the

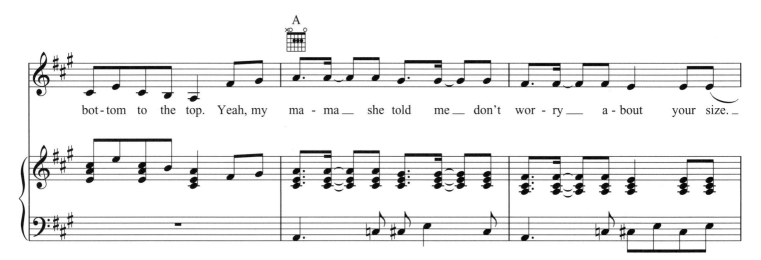

bot - tom to the top. Yeah, my ma - ma __ she told me __ don't wor - ry __ a - bout your size. __

She says, "Boys like __ a lit - tle __ more

boo - ty __ to hold at night." __ You know I

won't be __ no stick fig - ure, sil - i - cone Bar - bie doll. __

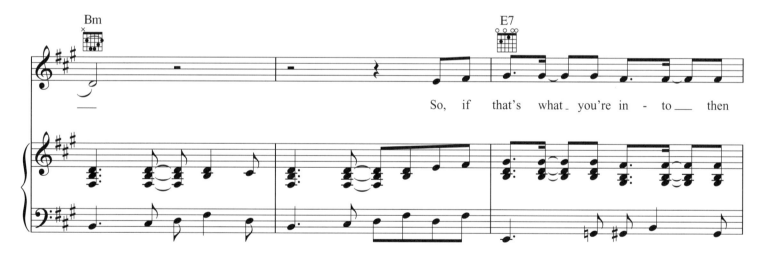

So, if that's what __ you're in - to __ then

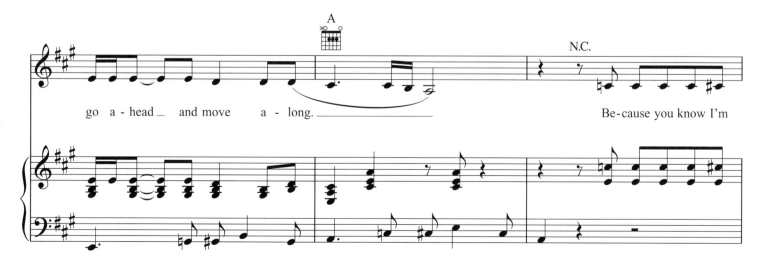

go a - head __ and move a - long. _____ Be-cause you know I'm

all a-bout that bass, 'bout that bass. No tre-ble. I'm all a-bout that bass, 'bout that

bass. No tre-ble. I'm all a-bout that bass, 'bout that bass. No tre-ble. I'm

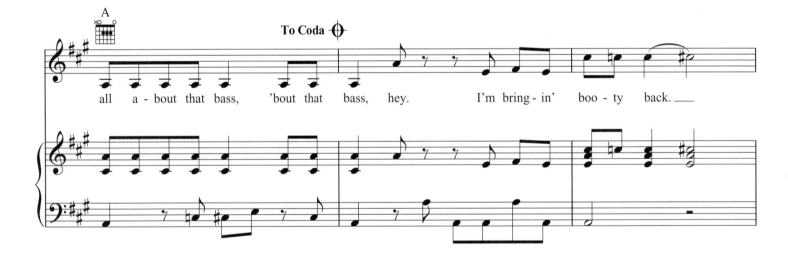

To Coda ⊕

all a-bout that bass, 'bout that bass, hey. I'm bring-in' boo-ty back. ___

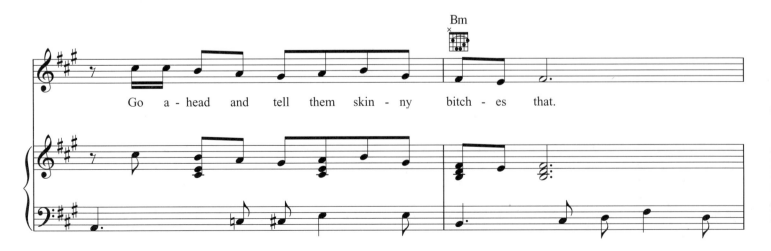

Go a-head and tell them skin-ny bitch-es that.

Nah, ___ I'm just playin'. I know you think you're fat. ___

D.S. al Coda

But I'm here to tell ya ev - 'ry

CODA

bass. Be - cause you know I'm

all a - bout that bass, 'bout that bass. No tre - ble. I'm all a - bout that bass, 'bout that

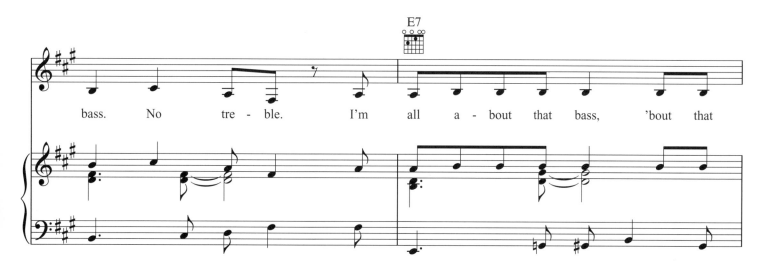

bass. No tre - ble. I'm all a - bout that bass, 'bout that

bass. No tre - ble. I'm all a - bout that bass, 'bout that bass. Be-cause you know I'm

bass.

AIN'T NO SUNSHINE

Words and Music by
BILL WITHERS

gone,
gone,
won-der if___ she's_ gone to stay.
on-ly dark-ness___ ev-'ry day.

Ain't no sun-shine when she's gone,_____ and this house just ain't no

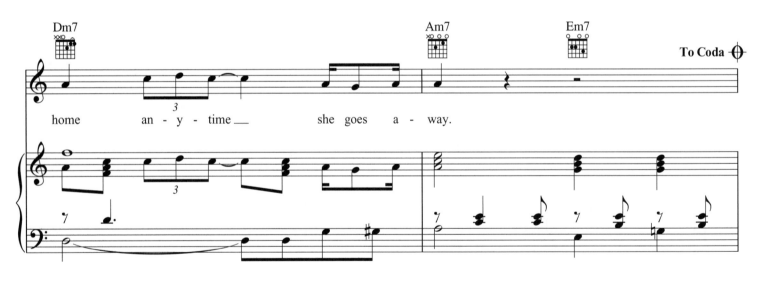

To Coda ⊕

home an-y-time___ she goes a-way.

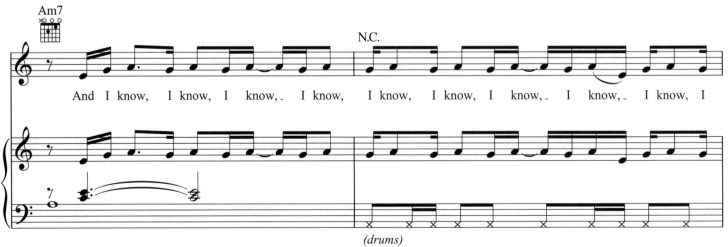

And I know, I know, I know,_ I know, I know, I know, I know,_ I know, I know, I

(drums)

ALL ALONG THE WATCHTOWER

Words and Music by
BOB DYLAN

Moderate Rock

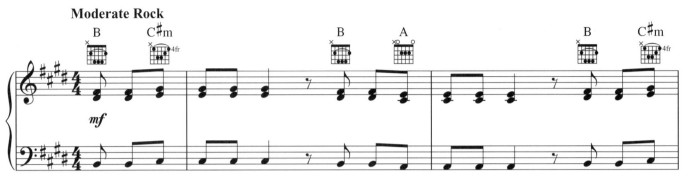

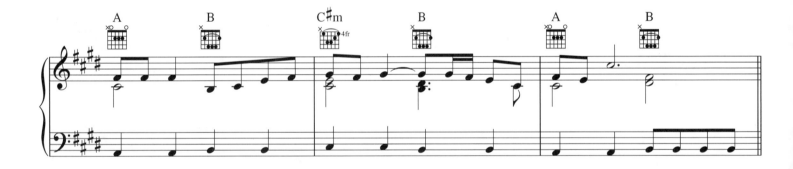

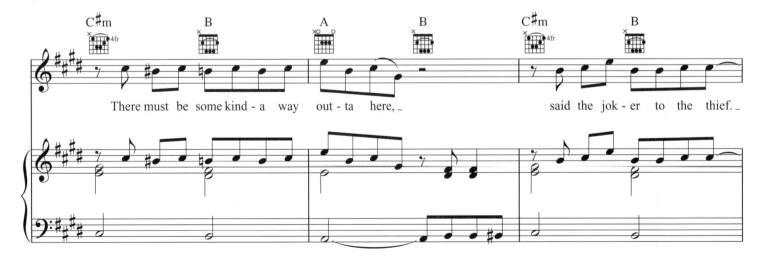

There must be some kind-a way out-ta here, ___ said the jok-er to the thief. ___

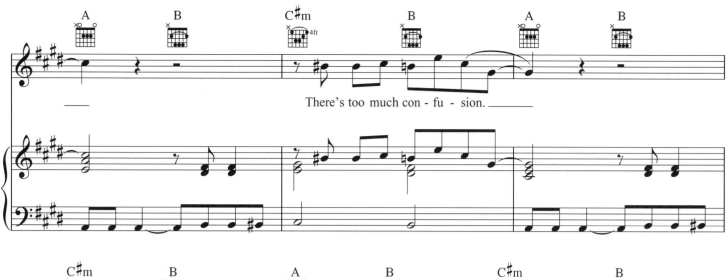

There's too much con - fu - sion.

I can't get no re - lief. _____ Busi-ness men they, ah, ah,

drink my wine. _____ Plow men dig my earth. _____

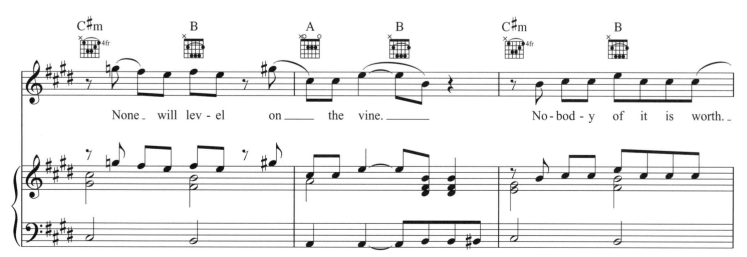

None _ will lev - el on _____ the vine. _____ No - bod - y of it is worth. _

Hey, _____ hey. No rea-son to get ex-cit-ed,

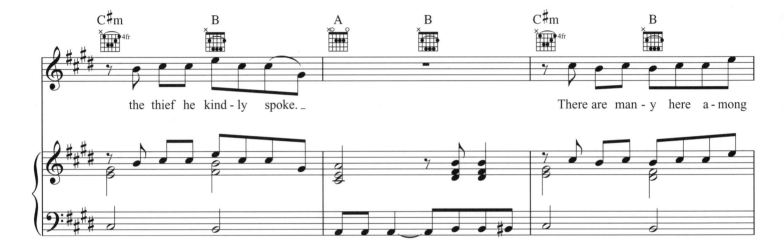

the thief he kind-ly spoke. _ There are man-y here a-mong

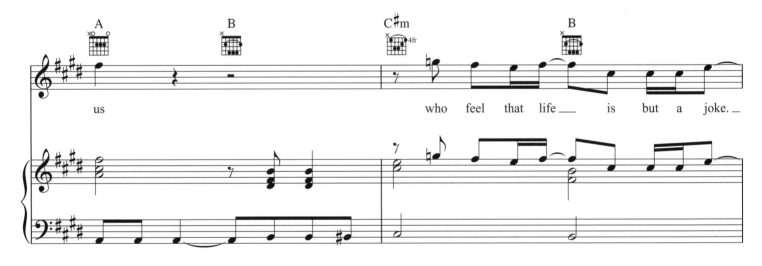

us who feel that life _ is but a joke. _

_ But, uh, but you and I, we've been _____

through that, but, uh, and this is not our fate.

_____ So let us not talk false - ly now.

The ho - ur's get - tin' ___ late. ___ Hey, well, all a - long ___ the watch-

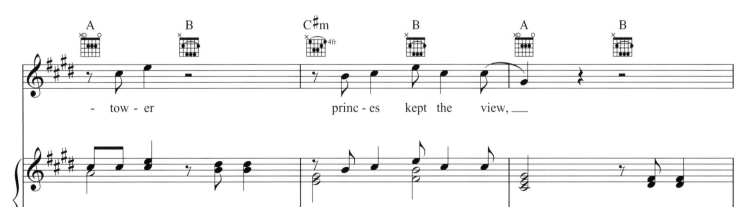

-tow - er princ - es kept the view, ___

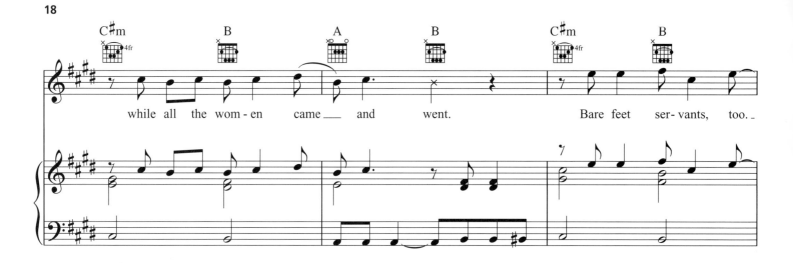

while all the wom-en came ___ and went. Bare feet ser-vants, too. ___

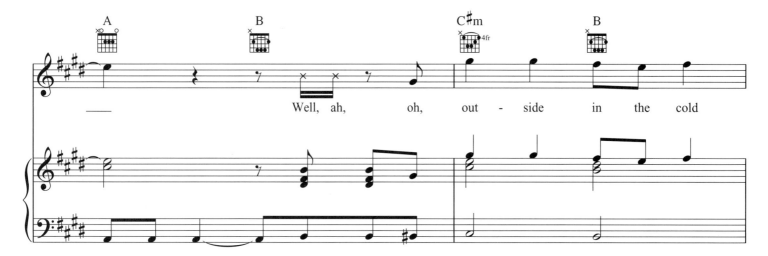

___ Well, ah, oh, out-side in the cold

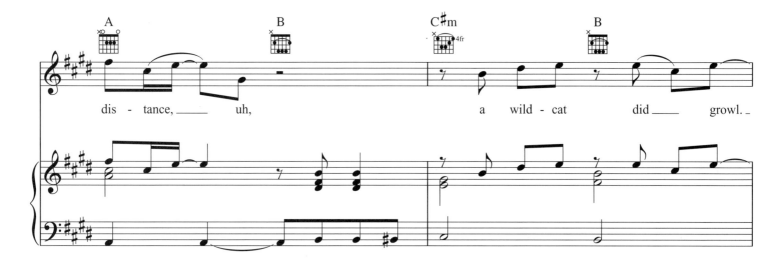

dis - tance, ___ uh, a wild-cat did ___ growl. ___

___ Two rid-ers were ap-proach-in', ___ and the

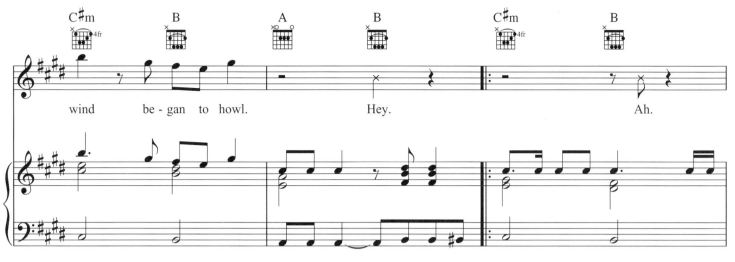

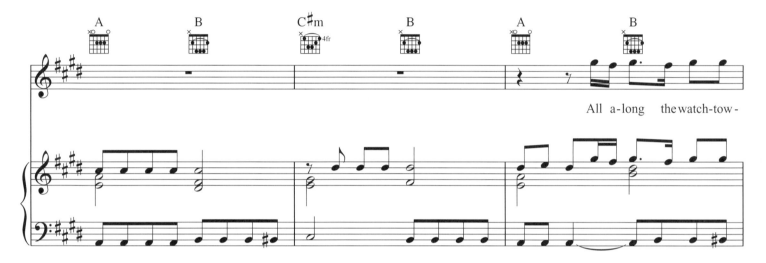

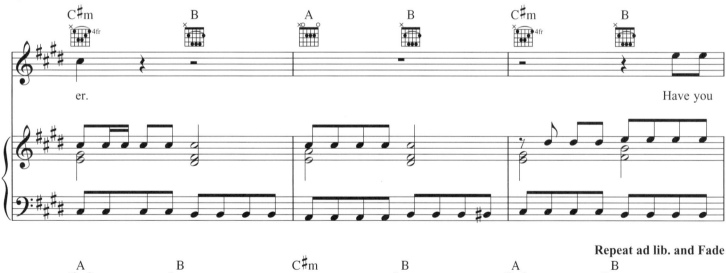

ALL APOLOGIES

Words and Music by
KURT COBAIN

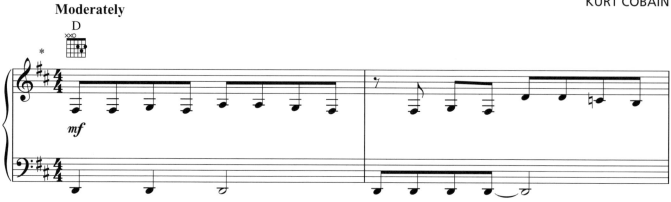

What else _____ should I _____ be? _____
I wish _____ I was like you, _____

Recorded a half step lower.

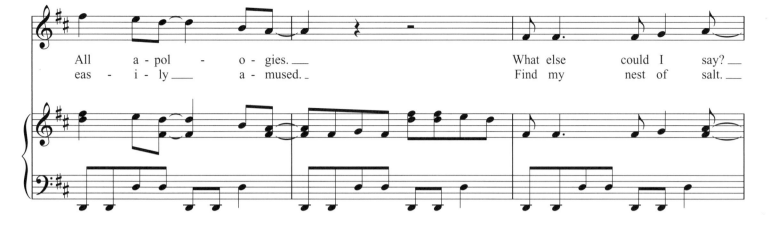

All a - pol - o - gies. ___ What else could I say? ___
eas - i - ly ___ a - mused. ___ Find my nest of salt. ___

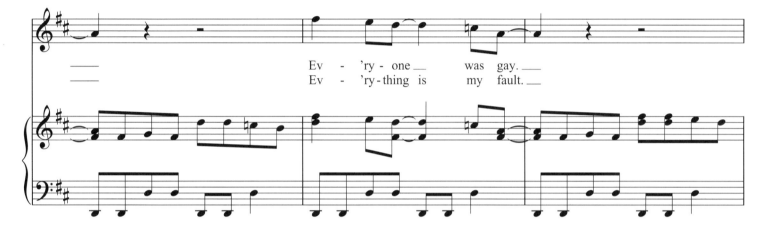

___ Ev - 'ry - one ___ was gay. ___
___ Ev - 'ry - thing is my fault. ___

What else could I write? ___ I don't have ___ the right. ___
I'll take all the blame, ___ a - qua sea - foam shame. ___

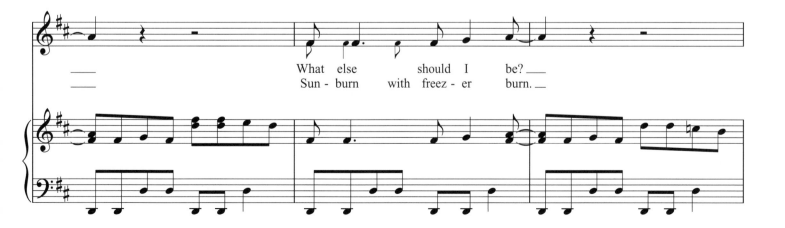

___ What else should I be? ___
___ Sun - burn with freez - er burn.

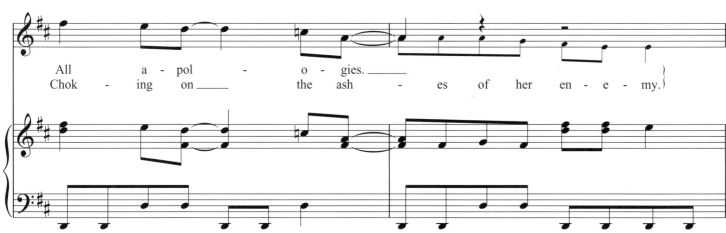

All a - pol - o - gies. ____
Chok - ing on ____ the ash - es of her en - e - my.

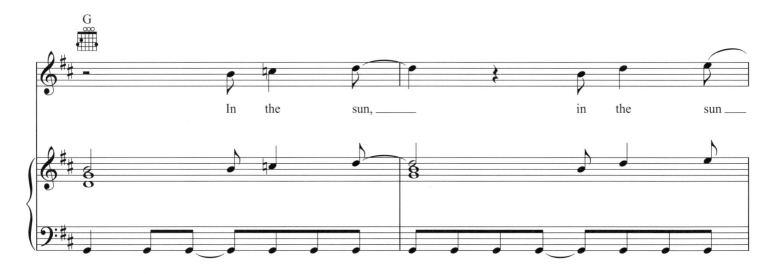

In the sun, ____ in the sun ____

____ I feel ____ as one. ____ In the sun, ____ in the sun ____

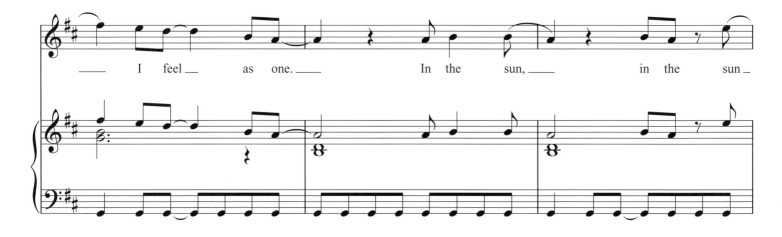

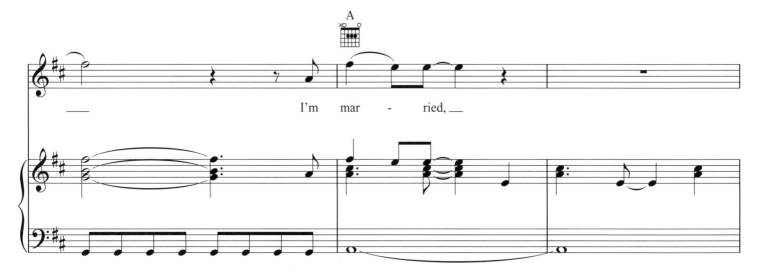

____ I'm mar - ried, ____

bur - ied. __
mar - ried. __

Mar - ried, __

bur - ied. __ Yeah yeah __ yeah yeah. __

D

All a - lone __ is all __ we all __ are.

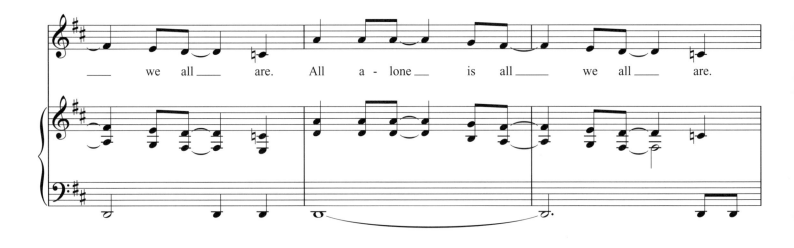

ALL RIGHT NOW

Words and Music by ANDY FRASER
and PAUL RODGERS

Moderately, with a strong beat

There she stood _____ in the
I took her home _____ to my

street _____ smil-ing from her head _____ to her feet. I said,
place _____ watch-ing ev-'ry move on her face. She said,

"Hey, _____ what is this?" _____ Now ba-by, may-be may-be she's in need _ of a
"Look, _____ what's your game, _____ ba-by, are you tryin' to put me in

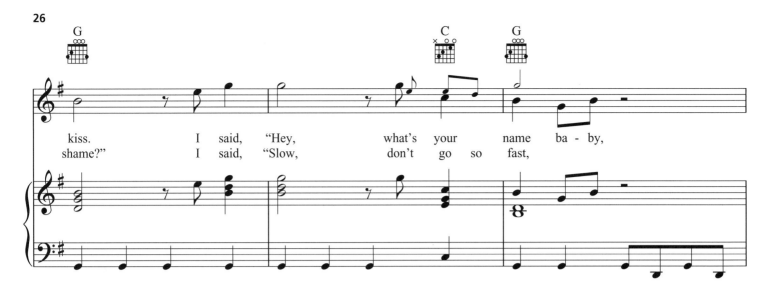

kiss.   I said, "Hey, what's your name ba - by,
shame?"   I said, "Slow, don't go so fast,

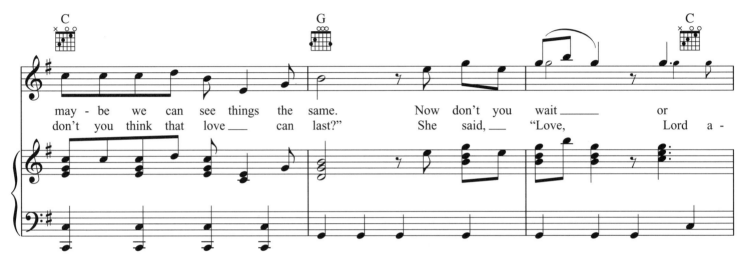

may - be we can see things the same. Now don't you wait _____ or
don't you think that love ___ can last?" She said, ___ "Love, ___ Lord a -

hes - i - tate, _____ let's move ___ be - fore they raise the park - ing
bove, _____ now ___ you're tryin' to trick me in

rate." }   All right now, _____ ba - by, it's all _____
love." }

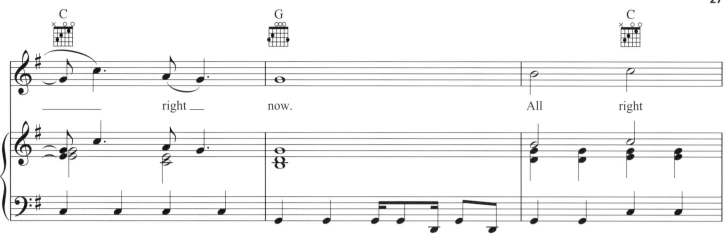

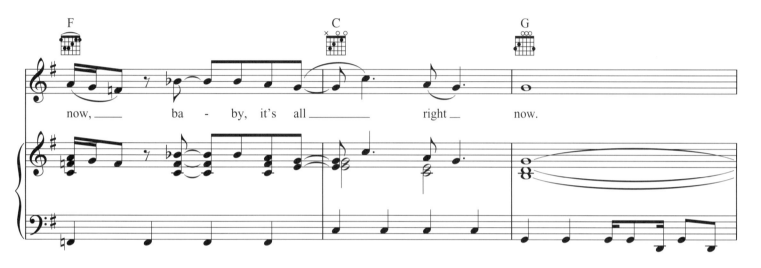

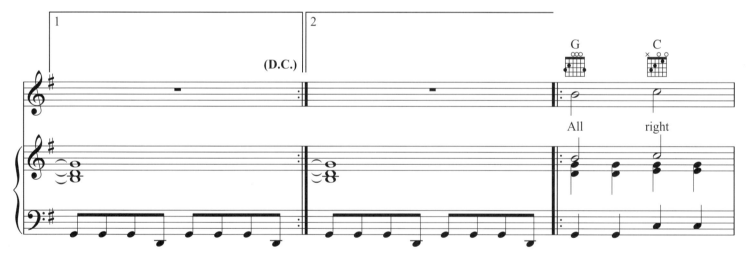

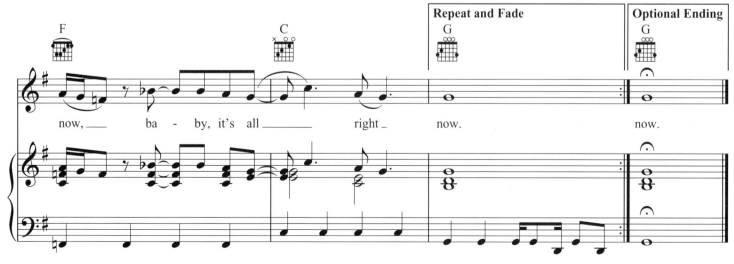

AUTHORITY SONG

Words and Music by
JOHN MELLENCAMP

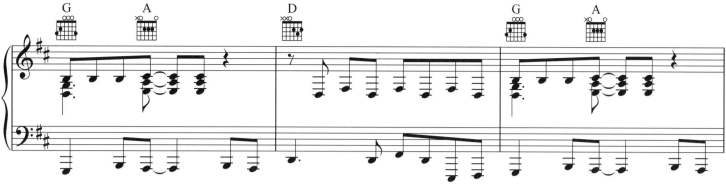

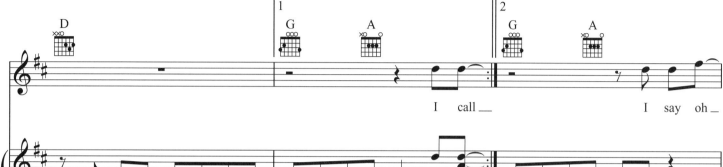

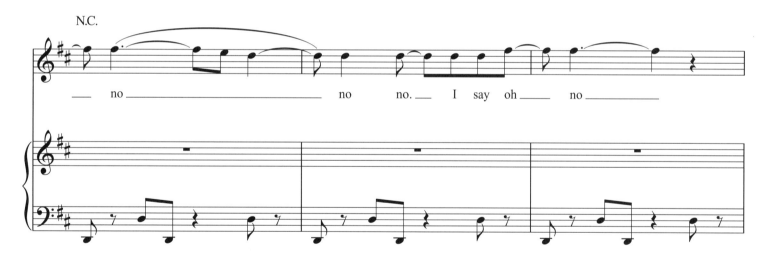

BEAT IT

Words and Music by
MICHAEL JACKSON

Moderately fast

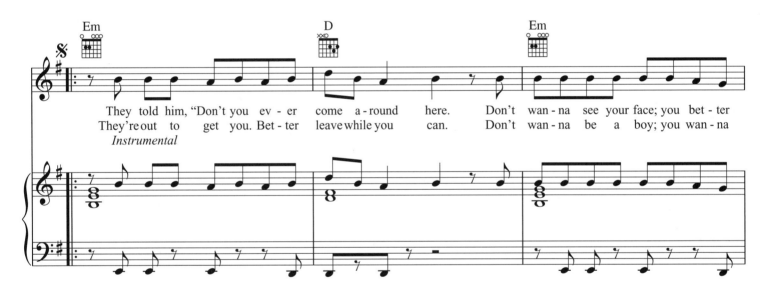

They told him, "Don't you ev-er come a-round here. Don't wan-na see your face; you bet-ter
They're out to get you. Bet-ter leave while you can. Don't wan-na be a boy; you wan-na

Instrumental

dis-ap-pear." The fi-re's in their eyes and their words are real-ly clear. So
be a man. You wan-na stay a-live; bet-ter do what you can. So

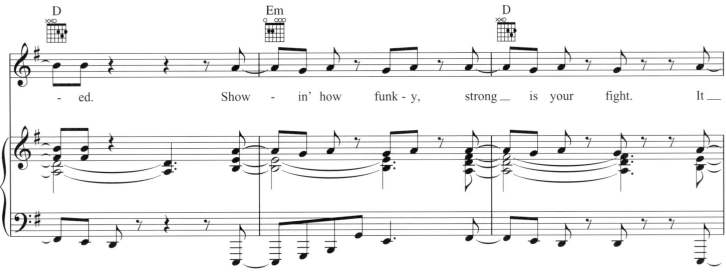

-ed. Show - in' how funk - y, strong __ is your fight. It __

__ does - n't mat - ter who's __ wrong or right. Just beat it. Beat it.

Beat it. Beat it.

D.S. al Coda

CODA

Em   D   Em

beat it,   beat it.   No ___ one wants to be de - feat -

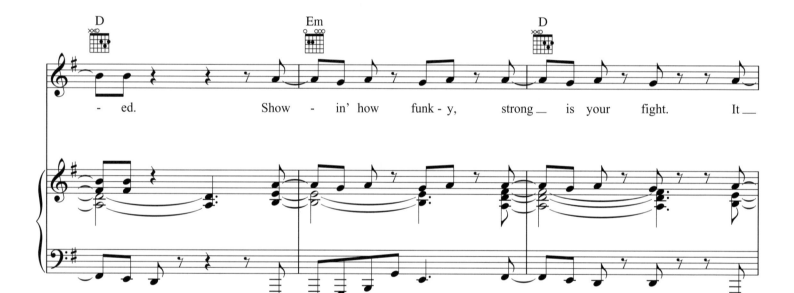

D   Em   D

- ed.   Show - in' how funk - y, strong __ is your fight. It __

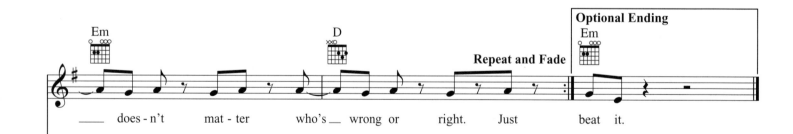

Em   D   **Repeat and Fade**   **Optional Ending**   Em

__ does - n't mat - ter who's __ wrong or right. Just beat it.

BLUE EYES CRYING IN THE RAIN

Words and Music by
FRED ROSE

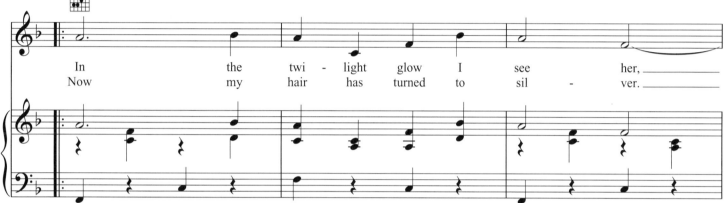

In the twi-light glow I see her,
Now my hair has turned to sil - ver.

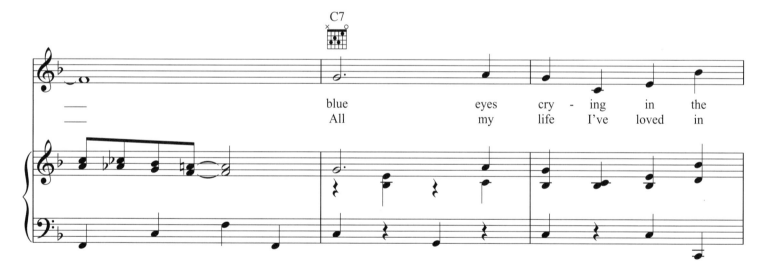

blue eyes cry-ing in the
All my life I've loved in

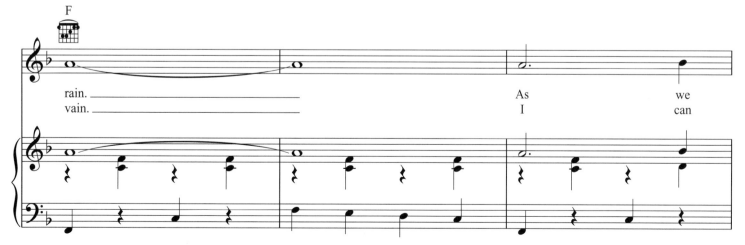

rain. As we
vain. I can

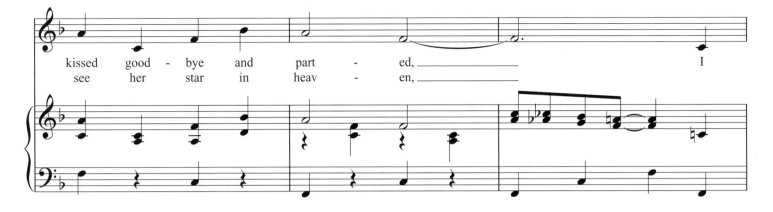

kissed good - bye and part - ed, _____ I
see her star in heav - en, _____

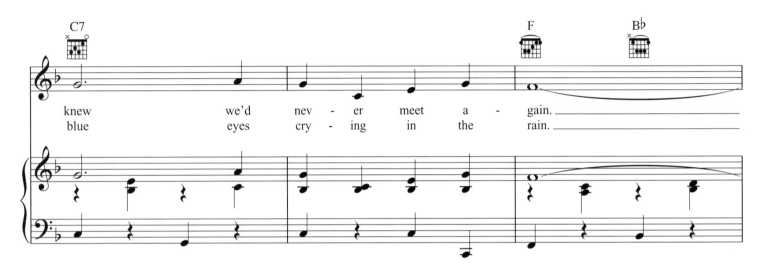

knew we'd nev - er meet a - gain. _____
blue eyes cry - ing in the rain. _____

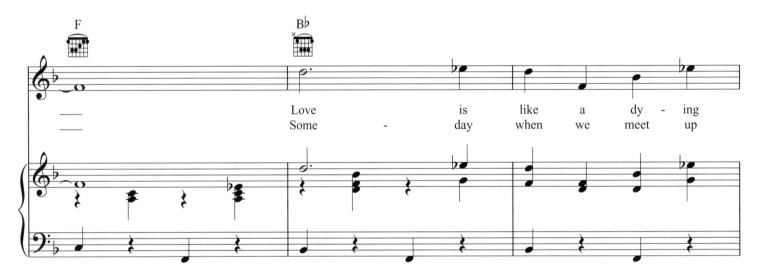

_____ Love is like a dy - ing
_____ Some - day when we meet up

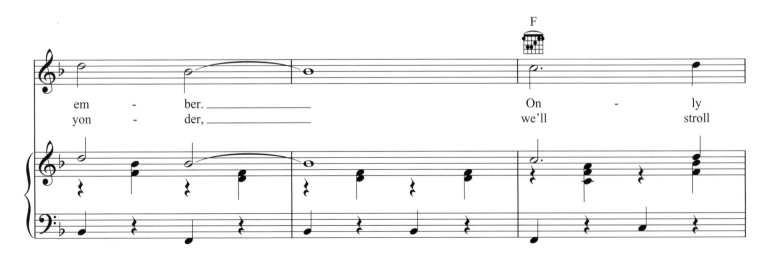

em - ber. _____ On - ly
yon - der, _____ we'll stroll

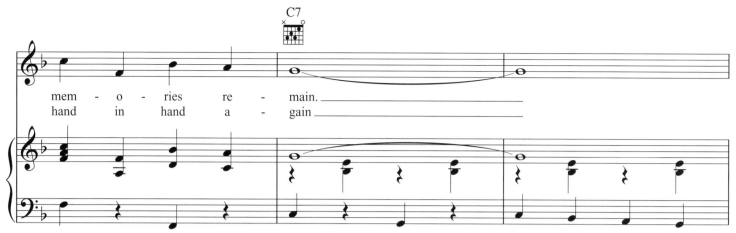

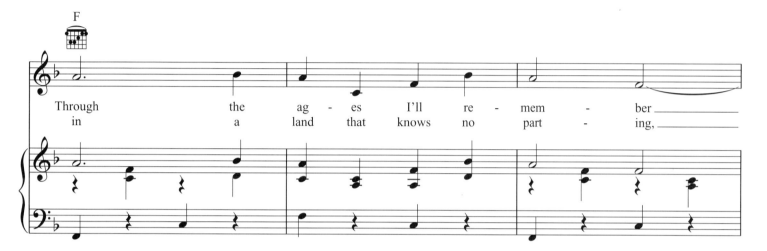

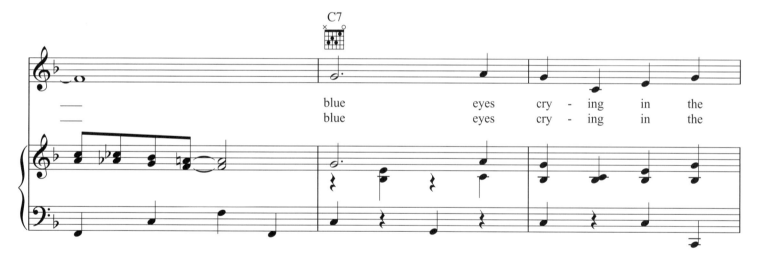

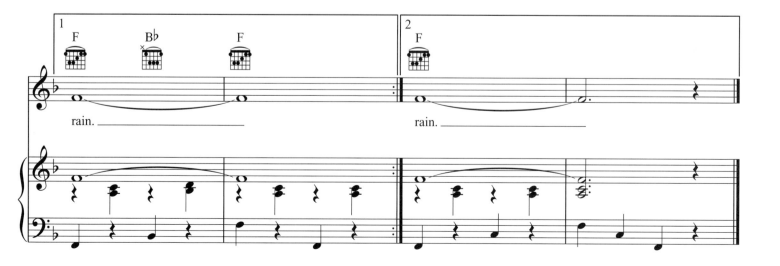

BYE BYE LOVE

Words and Music by FELICE BRYANT
and BOUDLEAUX BRYANT

Moderately fast

There goes my ba - by ____ with some - one
ro - mance, ____ I'm through with

new. ____ She sure looks hap - py; ____ I sure am
love. ____ I'm through with count - ing ____ the stars a -

blue. ____ She was my ba - by ____
bove. ____ And here's the rea - son ____

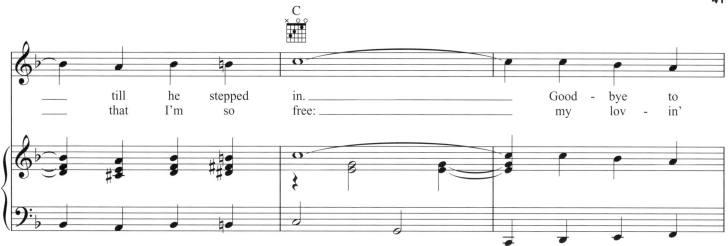

till he stepped in. _____ Good - bye to
that I'm so free: _____ my lov - in'

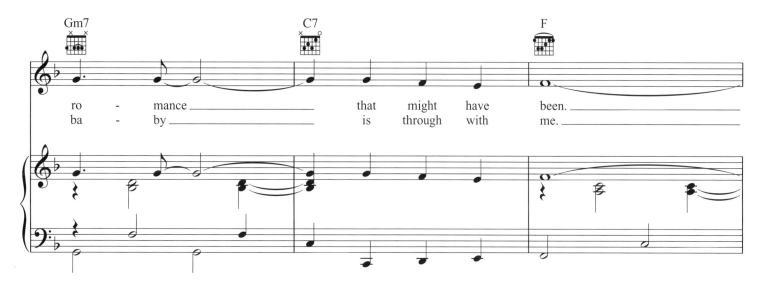

ro - mance _____ that might have been. _____
ba - by _____ is through with me. _____

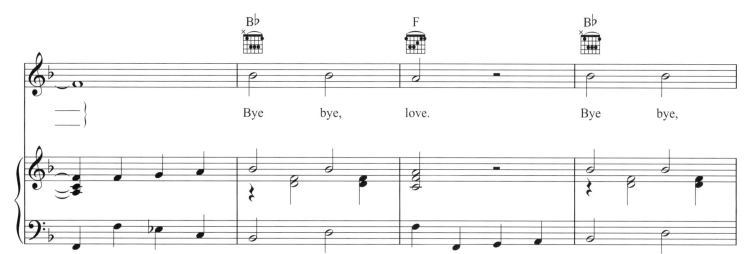

Bye bye, love. Bye bye,

hap - pi - ness. ___ Hel - lo, lone - li - ness; ___ I

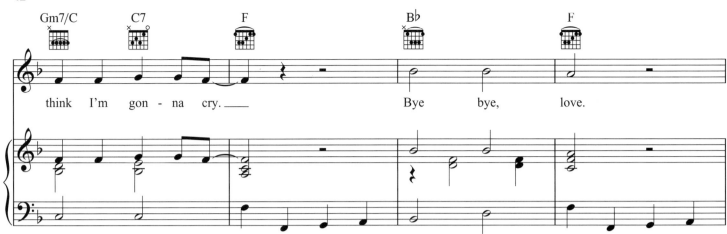

think I'm gon-na cry. _____ Bye bye, love.

Bye bye, sweet ca-ress. _ Hel-lo, emp-ti-ness; _ I

feel like I could die. _____ Bye bye, my love, good-

bye. I'm through with bye.

CHASING CARS

Words and Music by GARY LIGHTBODY,
TOM SIMPSON, PAUL WILSON,
JONATHAN QUINN and NATHAN CONNOLLY

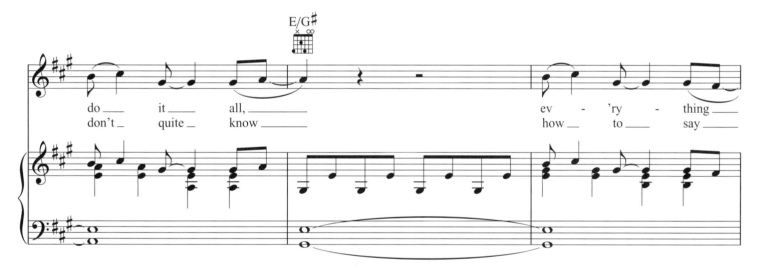

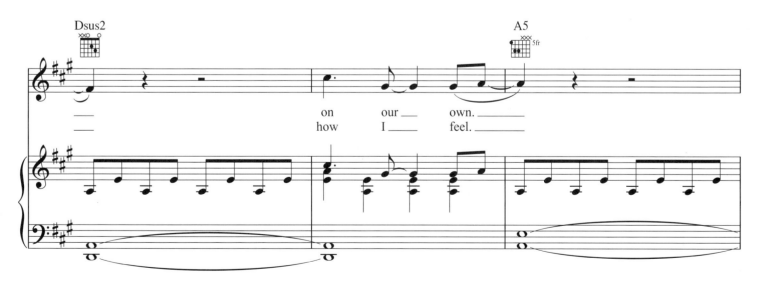

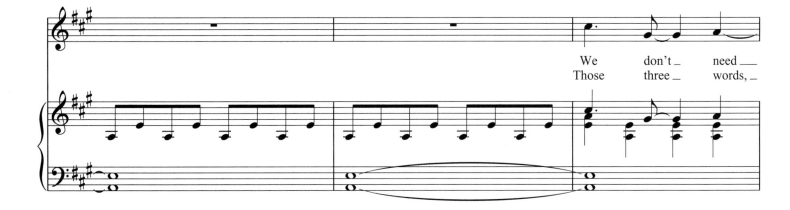

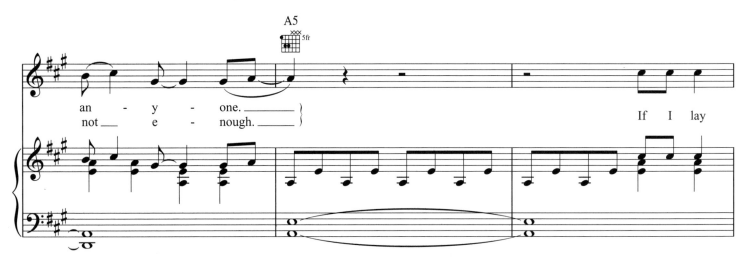

would you lie with me ___ and just for - get the world?

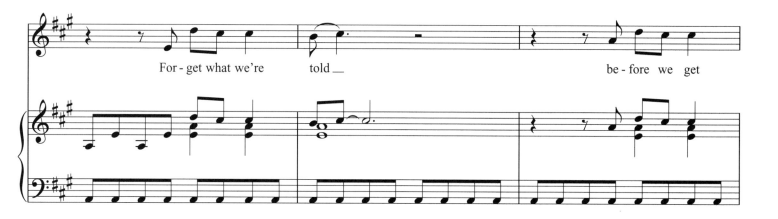

For - get what we're told ___ be - fore we get

too old. ___ Show me a gar - den ___ that's

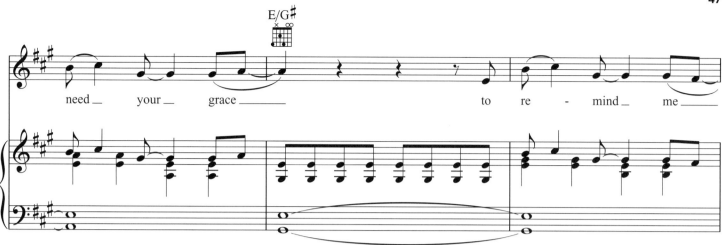

need __ your __ grace _____ to re - mind __ me _____

__ to find __ my __ own. _____

D.S. al Coda
(take 2nd ending)

If I lay

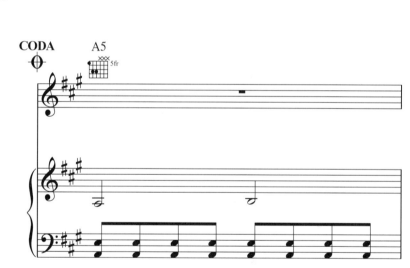

CODA

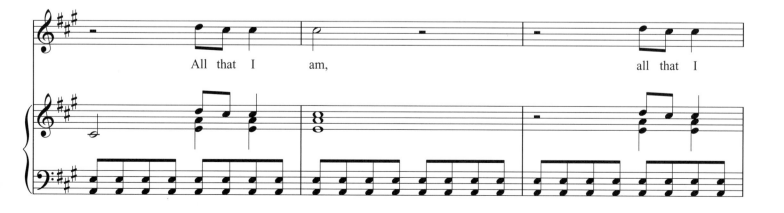

All that I am, all that I

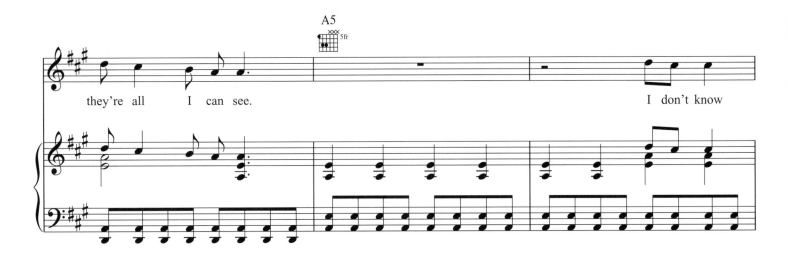

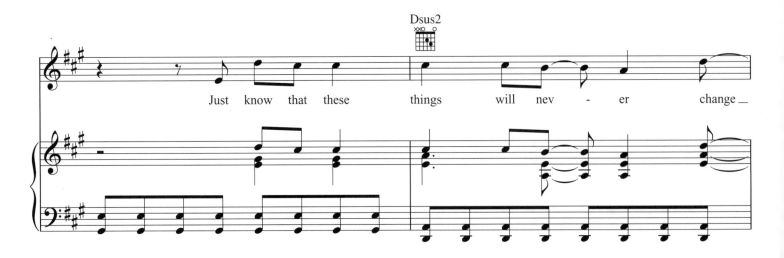

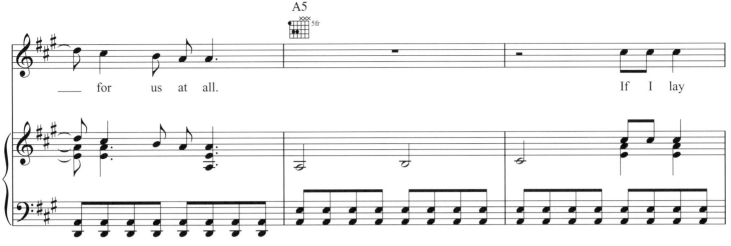

for us at all.

If I lay

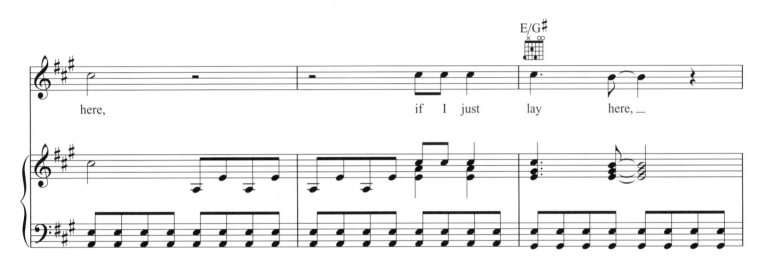

here,

if I just lay here, __

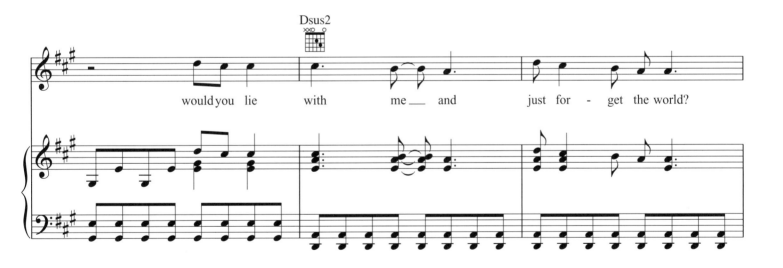

would you lie with me __ and

just for - get the world?

CECILIA

Words and Music by
PAUL SIMON

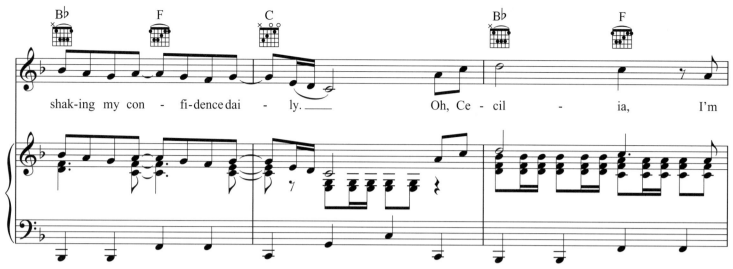

shak-ing my con - fi-dence dai - ly. ___ Oh, Ce - cil - ia, I'm

down on my knees, ___ I'm beg-ging you please ___ to come home. ___

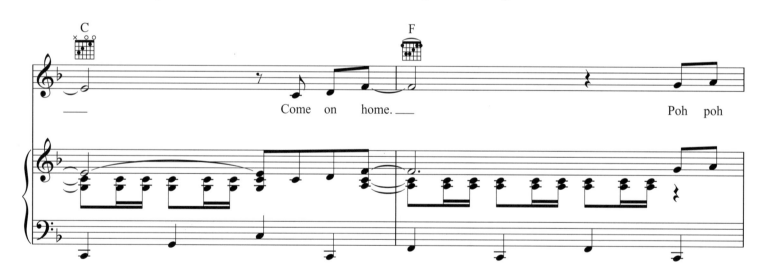

___ Come on home. ___ Poh poh

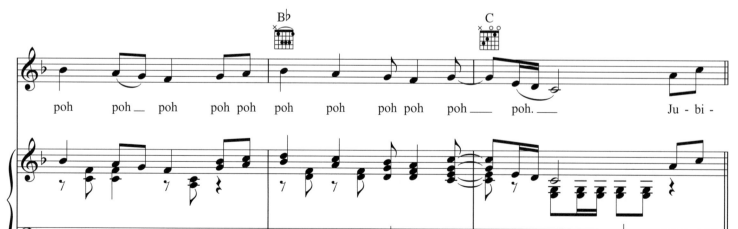

poh poh ___ poh poh poh poh poh poh poh poh ___ poh. ___ Ju - bi -

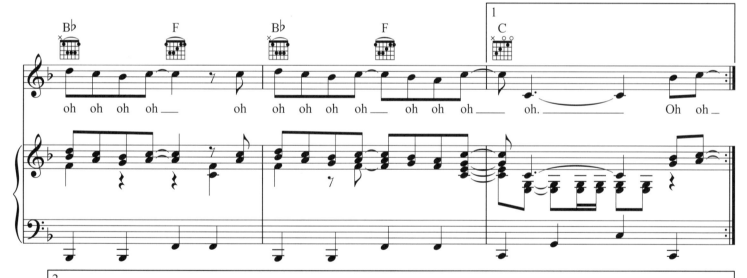

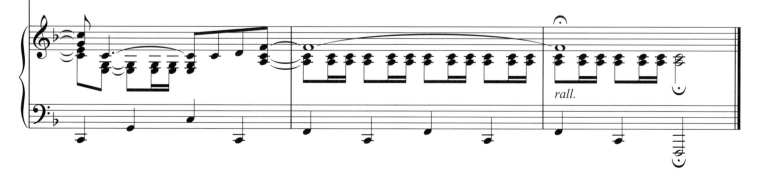

CHERRY, CHERRY

Words and Music by
NEIL DIAMOND

To Coda ⊕

Tell your ma - ma, girl, ___ I can't stay long.
No, we won't ___ tell a soul ___ where we gone to.

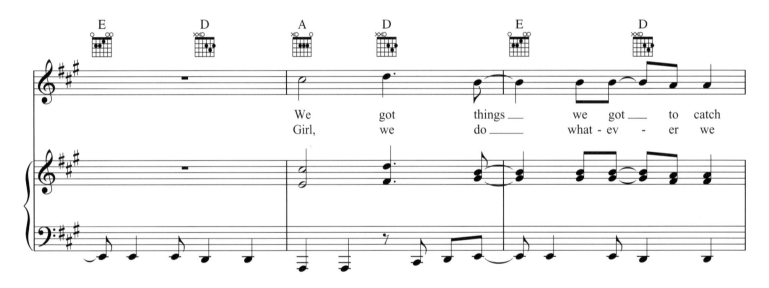

We got things ___ we got ___ to catch
Girl, we do ___ what - ev - er we

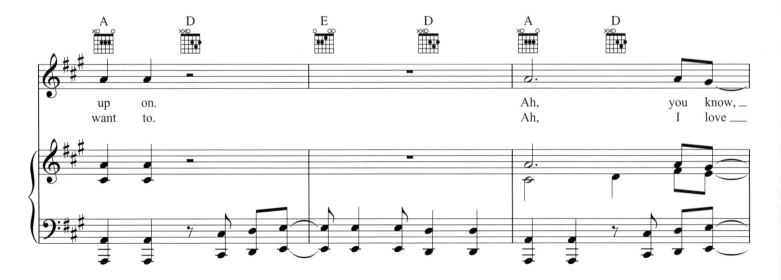

up on. Ah, you know, ___
want to. Ah, I love ___

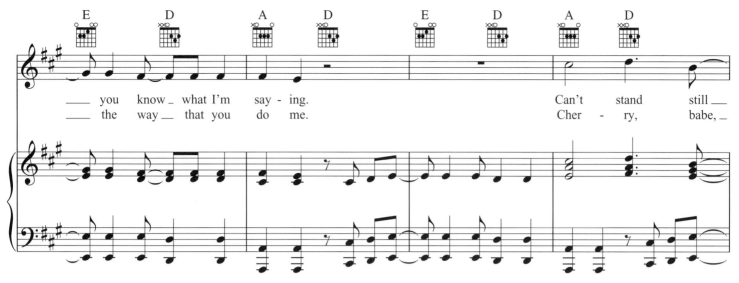

you know __ what I'm say - ing.
the way __ that you do me.
Can't stand still __
Cher - ry, babe, __

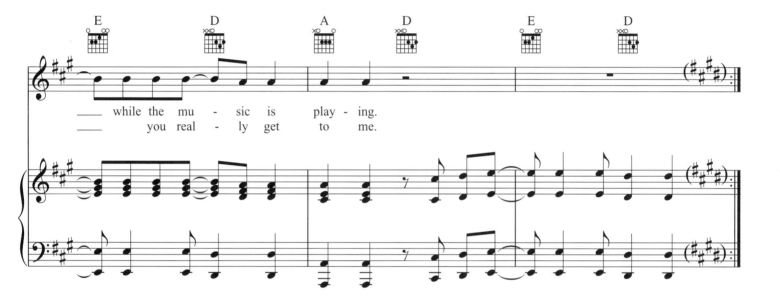

__ while the mu - sic is play - ing.
__ you real - ly get to me.

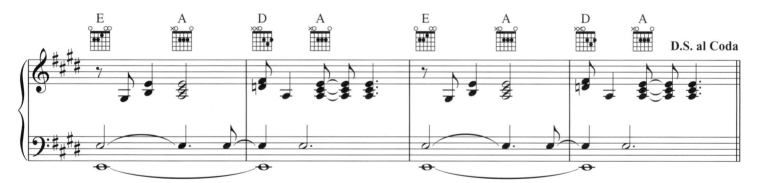

D.S. al Coda

CODA

N.C.

8va

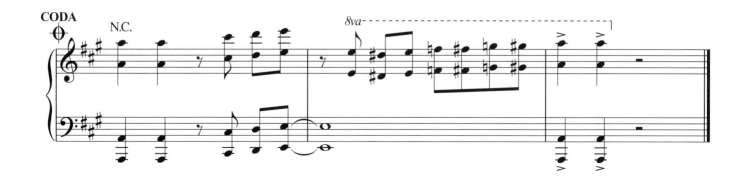

CLOSER TO FREE

Words and Music by SAM LLANAS
and KURT NEUMANN

Fast driving Rock

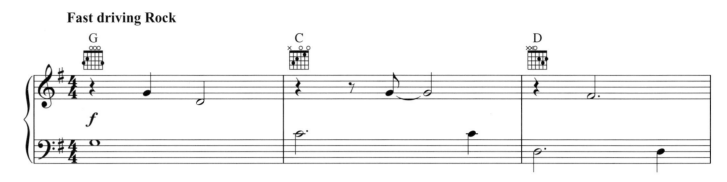

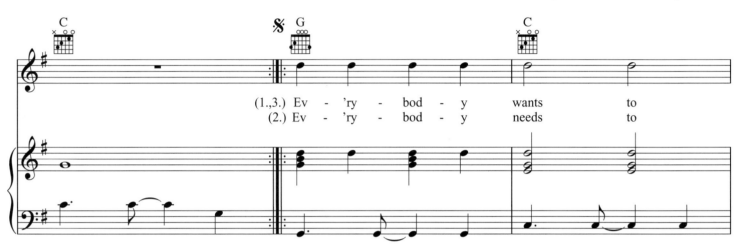

(1.,3.) Ev - 'ry - bod - y wants to
(2.) Ev - 'ry - bod - y needs to

live, like they want to live ___ and ev - 'ry - bod - y
touch, you know now and then. ___ And ev - 'ry - bod - y

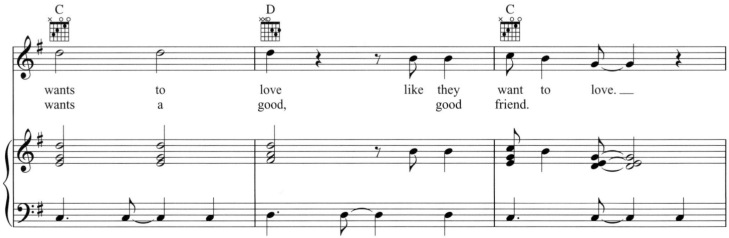

wants to love like they want to love. ___
wants a good, good friend.

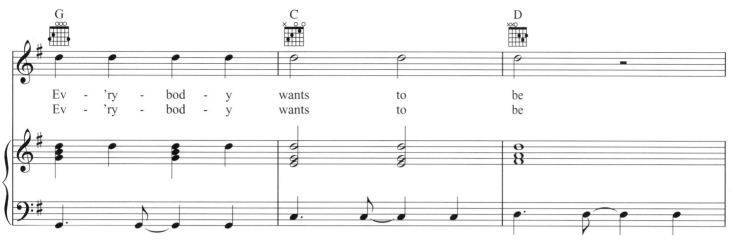

Ev - 'ry - bod - y wants to be
Ev - 'ry - bod - y wants to be

To Coda ⊕

clos - er ___ to ___ free.
clos - er ___ to ___ free.

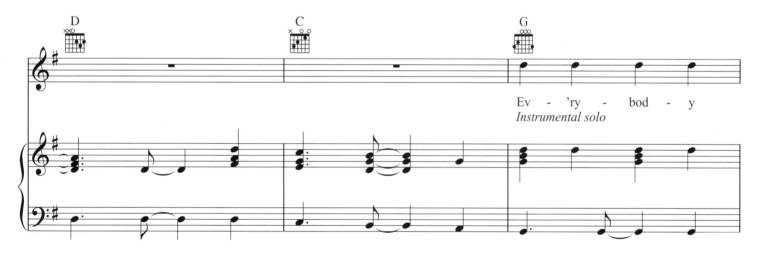

Ev - 'ry - bod - y
Instrumental solo

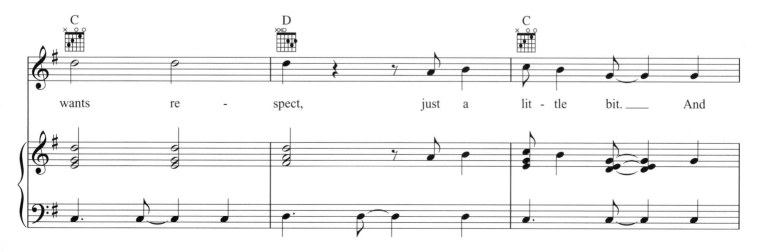

wants re - spect, just a lit - tle bit. ___ And

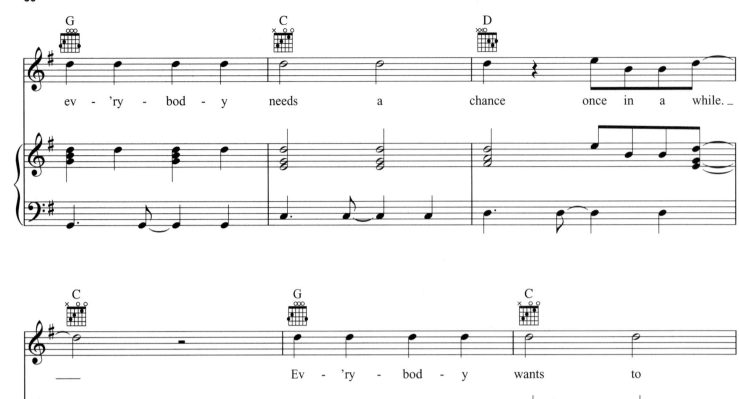

ev - 'ry - bod - y needs a chance once in a while. __

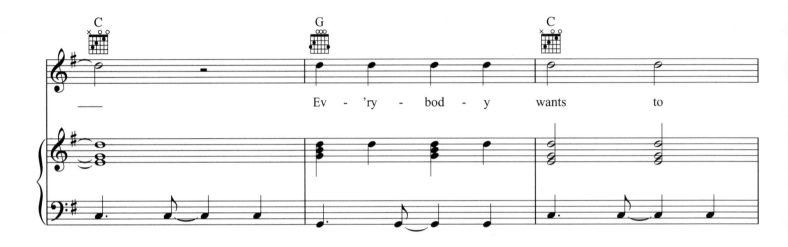

__ Ev - 'ry - bod - y wants to

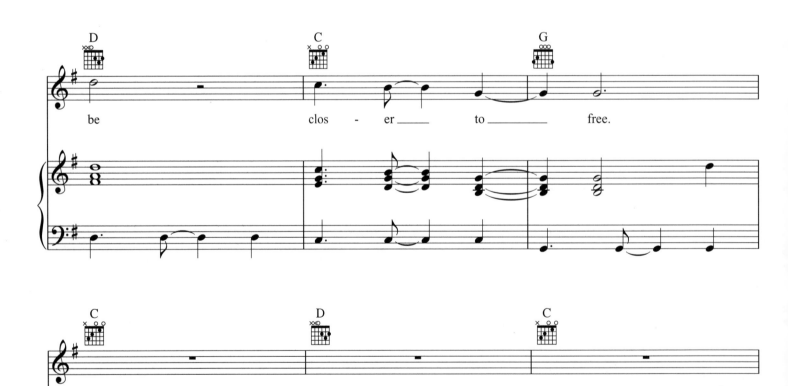

be clos - er __ to __ free.

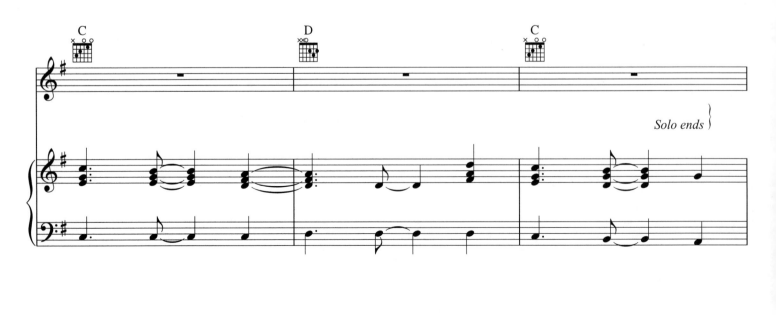

Solo ends

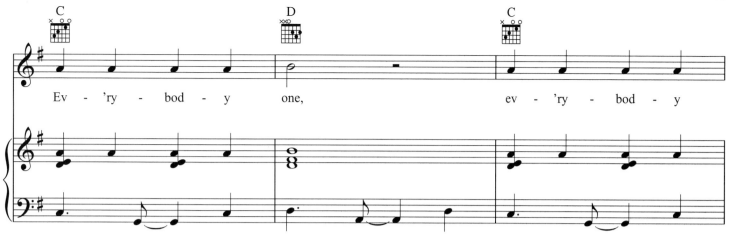

Ev - 'ry - bod - y one, ev - 'ry - bod - y

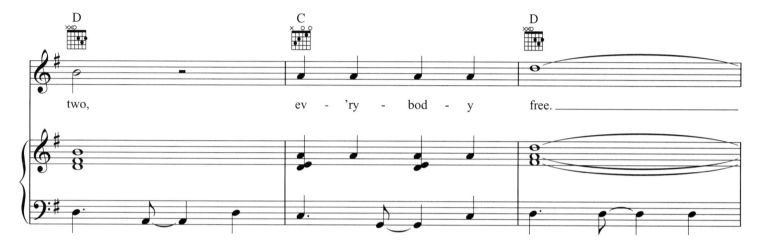

two, ev - 'ry - bod - y free. _____

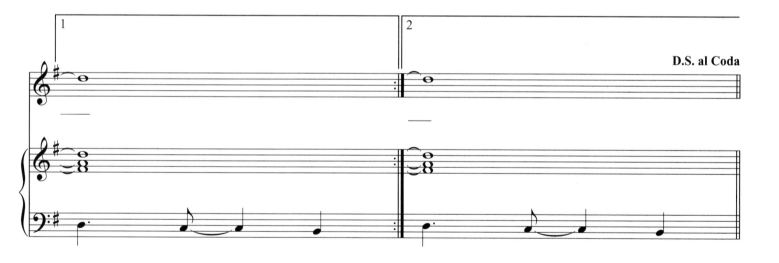

D.S. al Coda

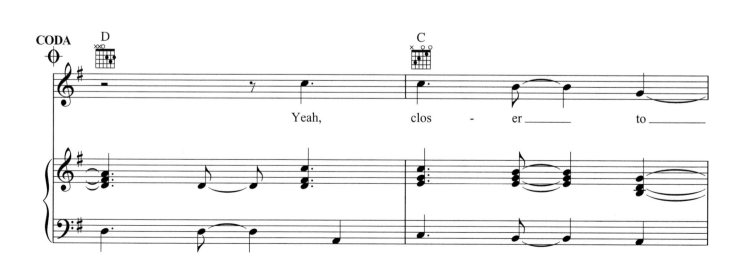

Yeah, clos - er _____ to _____

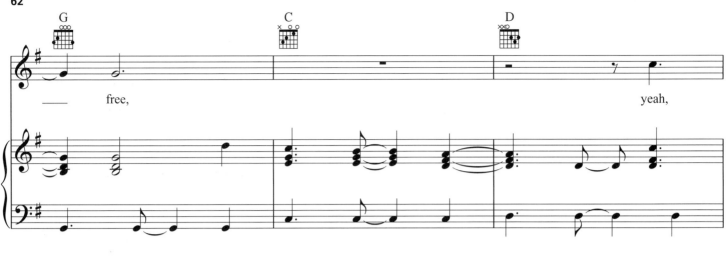

free,   yeah,

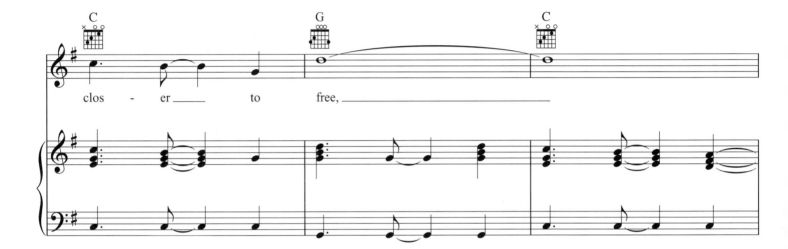

clos - er _____ to   free, _____

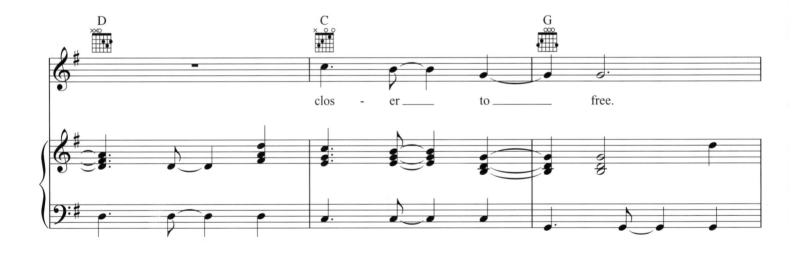

clos - er _____ to _____ free.

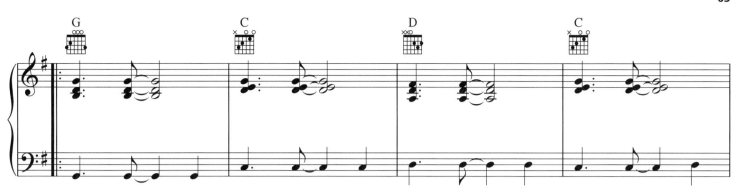

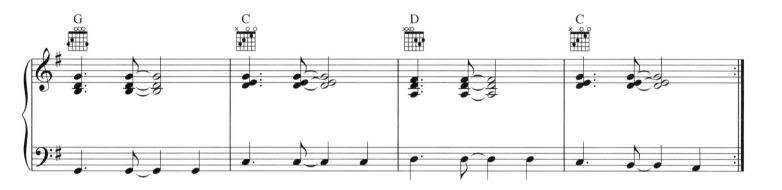

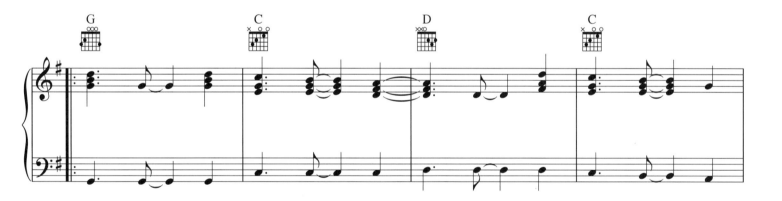

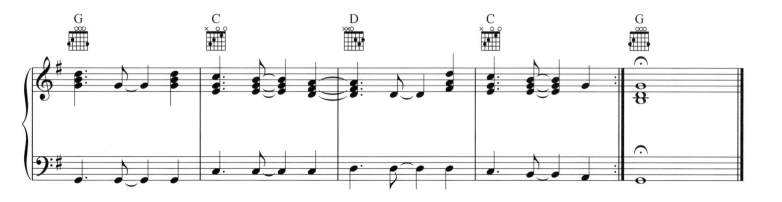

DOWN ON THE CORNER

Words and Music by
JOHN FOGERTY

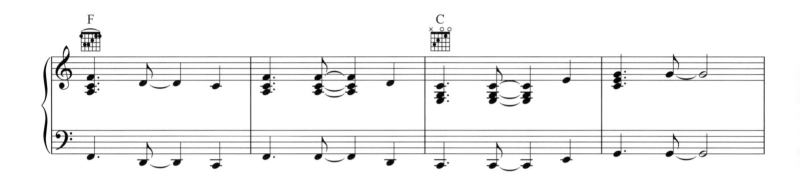

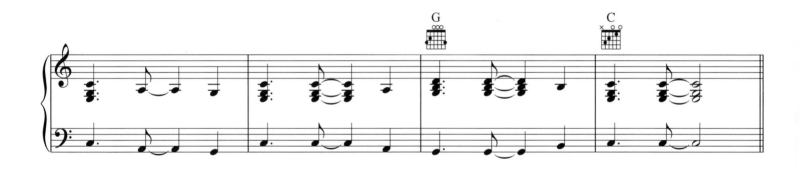

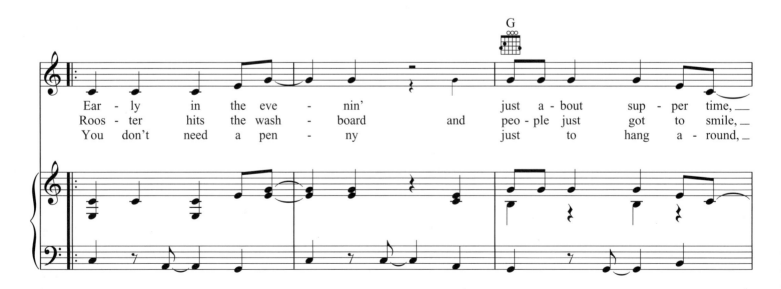

Ear- ly in the eve- nin' just a- bout sup- per time, ___
Roos- ter hits the wash- board and peo- ple just got to smile, ___
You don't need a pen- ny just to hang a- round, ___

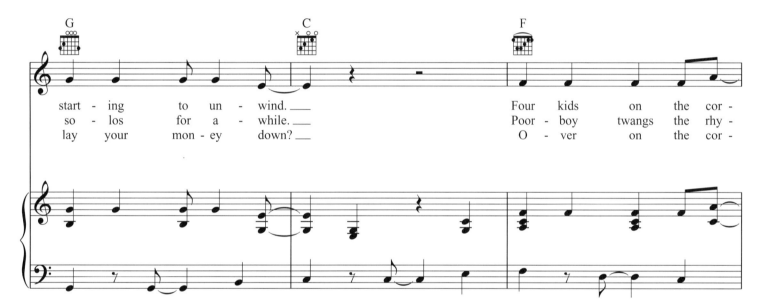

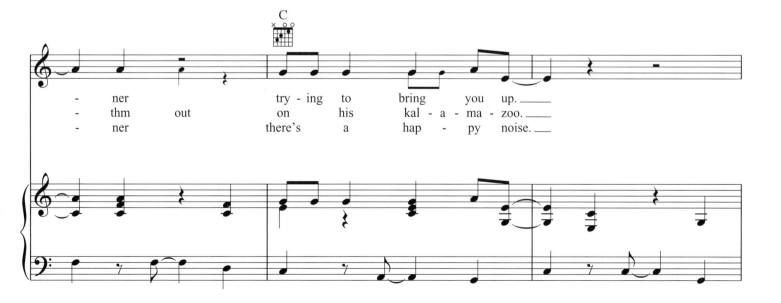

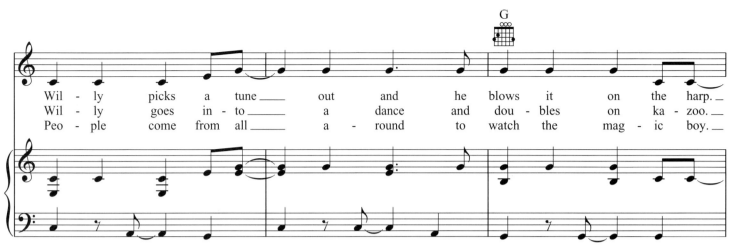

Wil - ly picks a tune ___ out and he blows it on the harp. ___
Wil - ly goes in - to ___ a dance and dou - bles on ka - zoo. ___
Peo - ple come from all ___ a - round to watch the mag - ic boy. ___

Down on the cor - ner,

out in the street, ___ Wil - ly and the Poor - boys are play -

D.S. and Fade

- in'. Bring a nick - el; tap your feet. ___

DREAMS

Words and Music by
STEVIE NICKS

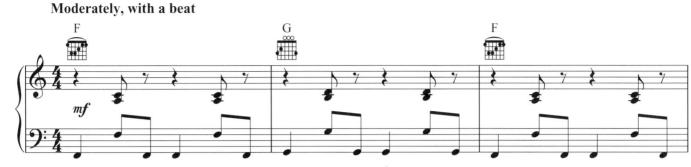

Moderately, with a beat

Now, here you go _____ a - gain. _____ You say
Now, here I go _____ a - gain. _____ I see

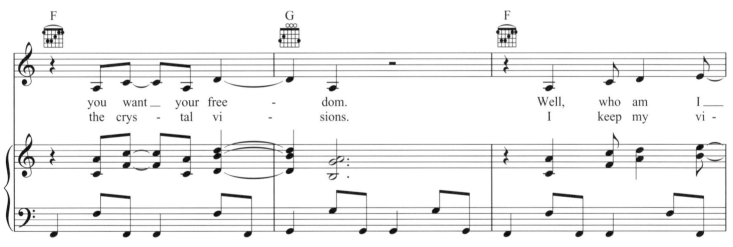

you want _____ your free - dom.
the crys - tal vi - sions.

Well, who am I _____
I keep my vi -

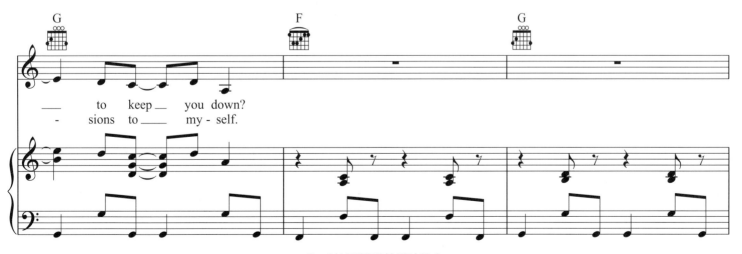

_____ to keep _____ you down?
- sions to _____ my - self.

It's on-ly right _____ that you _____ should play the way _____ you feel _____
It's on-ly me _____ who wants _____ to wrap a-round _____ your dreams. _____

_____ it. But lis-ten care-ful-ly _____ to the sound _____
_____ And have you an-y dreams _____ you'd like to sell? _____

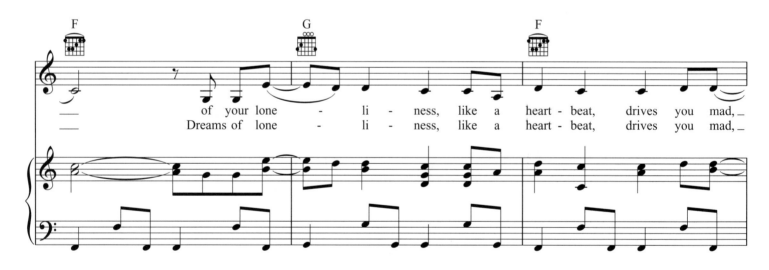

_____ of your lone - li - ness, like a heart-beat, drives you mad, _____
Dreams of lone - li - ness, like a heart-beat, drives you mad, _____

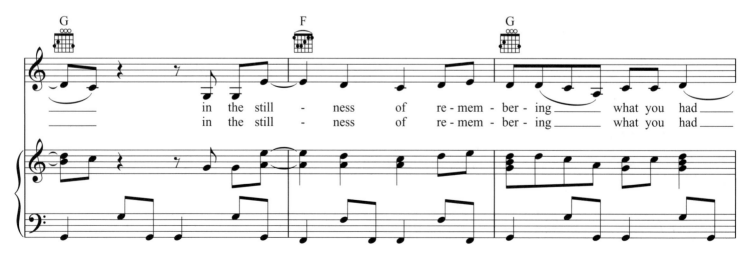

_____ in the still - ness of re-mem-ber-ing _____ what you had _____
_____ in the still - ness of re-mem-ber-ing _____ what you had _____

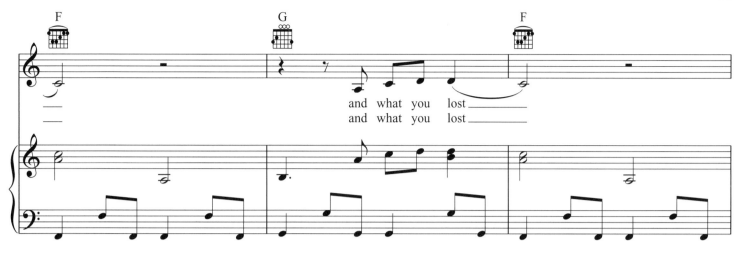

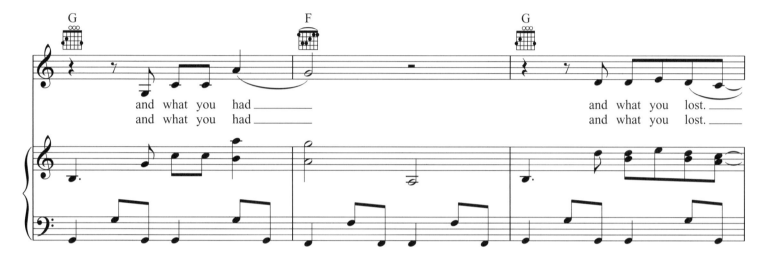

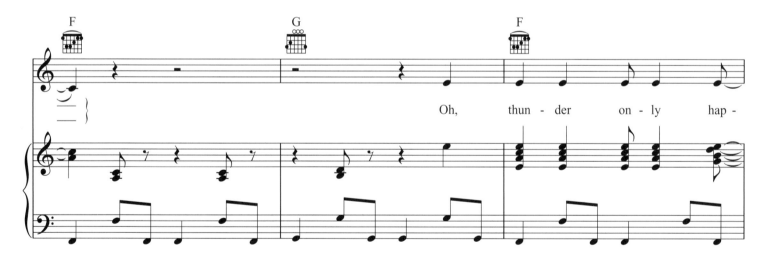

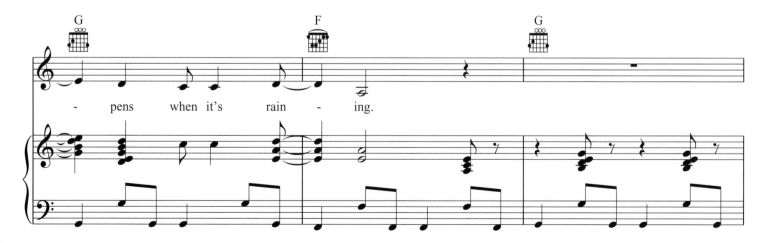

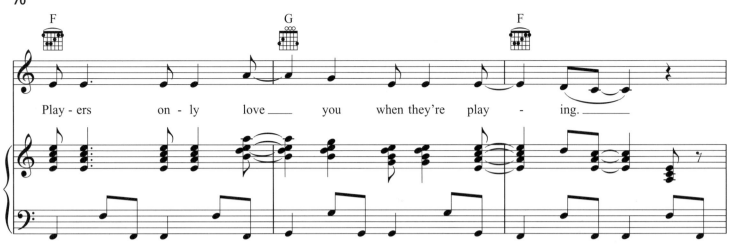

Play-ers on-ly love ___ you when they're play - ing. ___

Say, wom-en, they will come ___ and they will go. ___

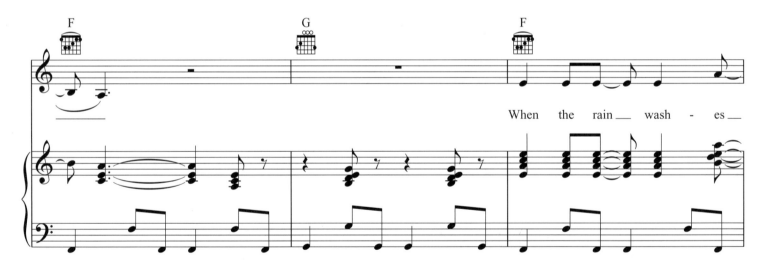

When the rain ___ wash - es ___

To Coda ⊕

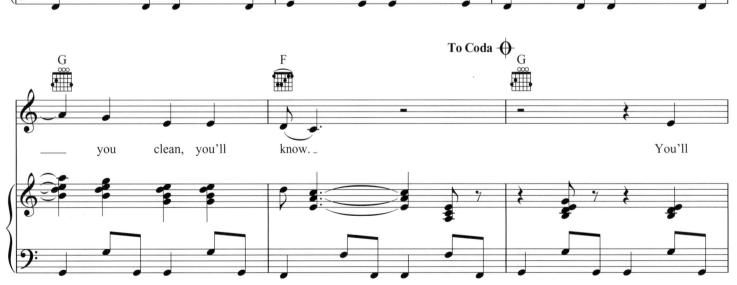

___ you clean, you'll know. ___ You'll

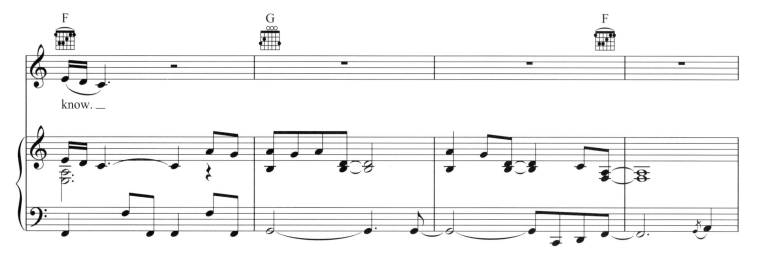

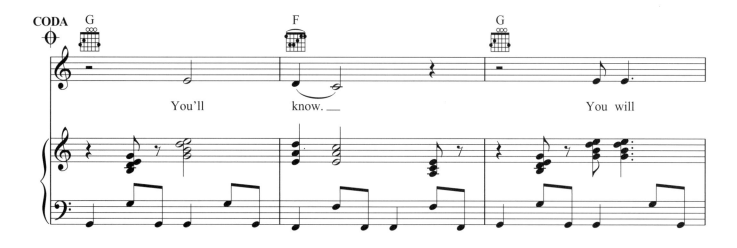

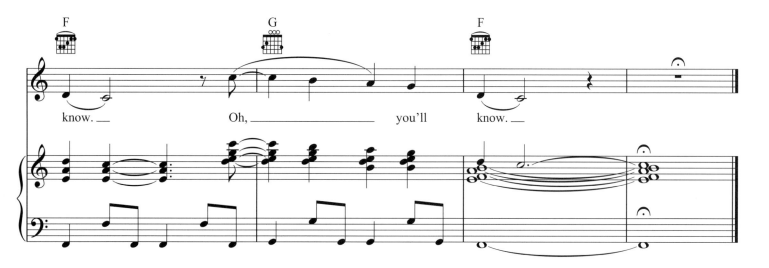

EVIL WAYS

Words and Music by
SONNY HENRY

Moderately

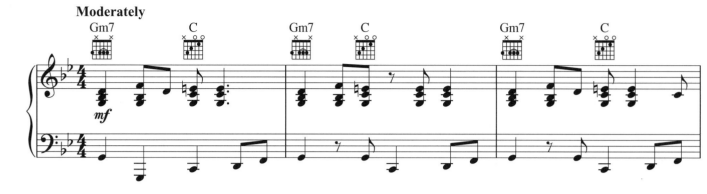

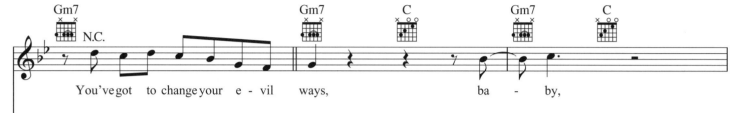

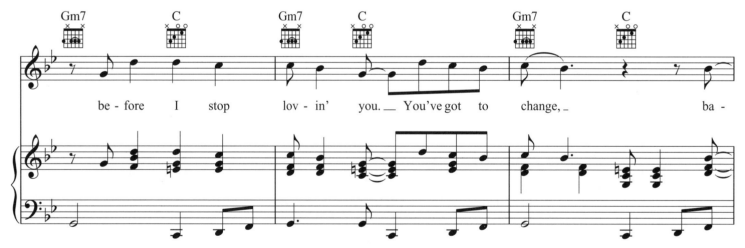

You've got to change your e - vil ways, ba - by,

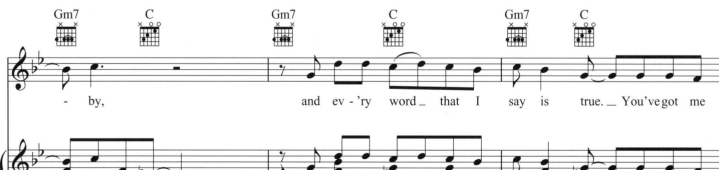

be - fore I stop lov - in' you. __ You've got to change, __ ba -

- by, and ev - 'ry word __ that I say is true. __ You've got me

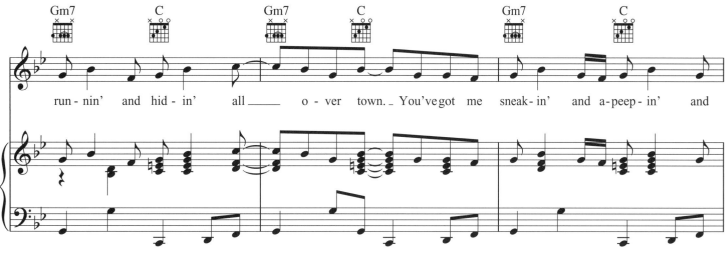

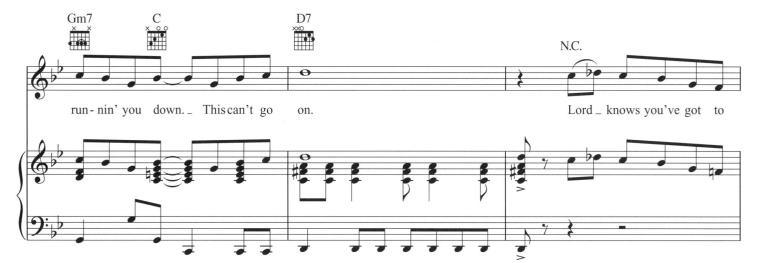

my house is dark __ and my thoughts are cold. __ You're hang-in' 'round, __ ba-

- by, with Jean and Joan __ and a - who knows who. __ I'm get-tin'

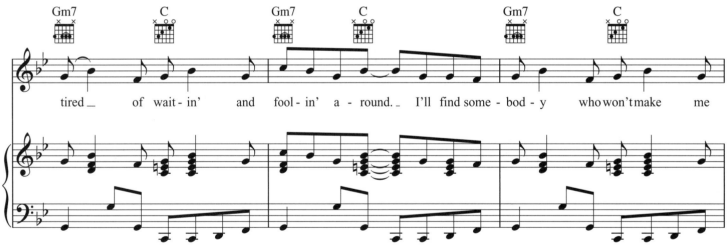

tired __ of wait-in' and fool-in' a - round. __ I'll find some - bod - y who won't make me

To Coda ⊕

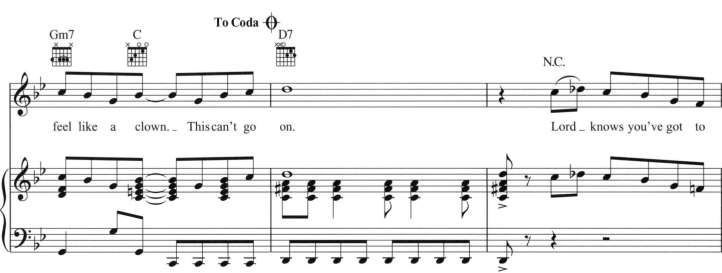

feel like a clown. __ This can't go on. Lord __ knows you've got to

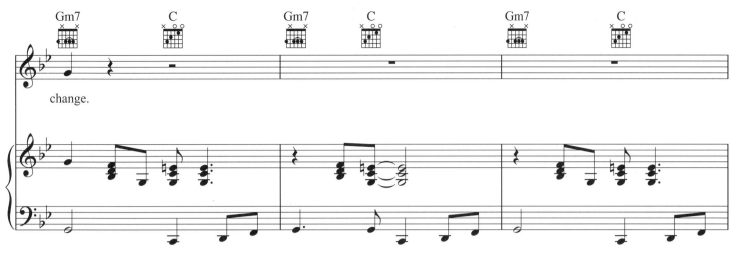

change.

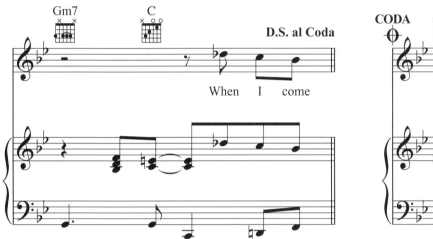

D.S. al Coda

When I come

CODA

on.

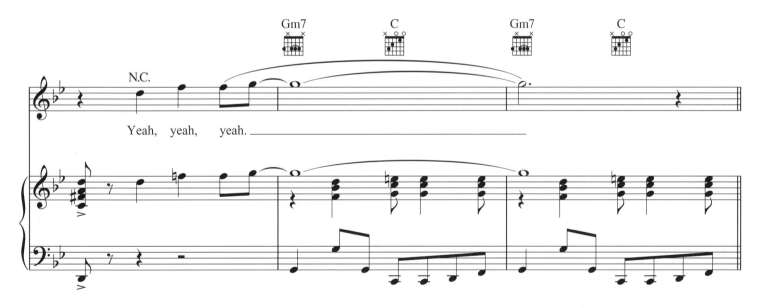

N.C.

Yeah, yeah, yeah.

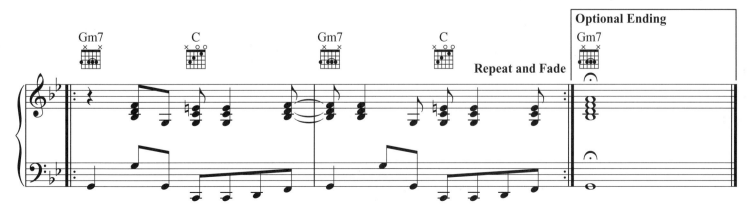

Optional Ending

Repeat and Fade

THE FIRST CUT IS THE DEEPEST

Words and Music by
CAT STEVENS

Slowly, with a beat

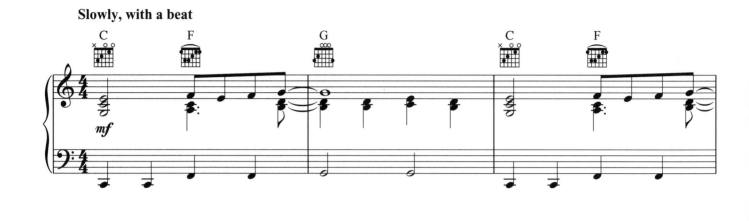

I would have giv-en you all ___ of my heart, ___ but there's
want ___ you by ___ my side, ___ just to

some-one who's torn it a-part. ___ And {she's}{he's} tak-en just all ___ that I had, ___
help me dry the tears that I've cried. ___ And I'm sure gon-na give you a try, ___

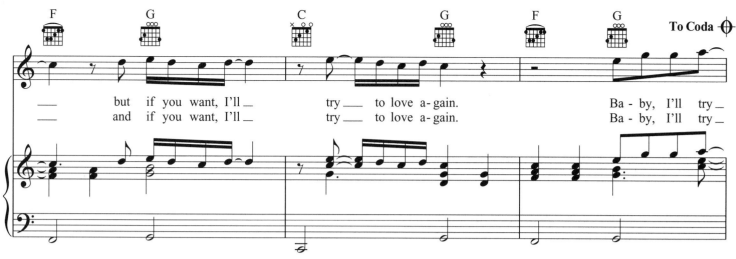

To Coda

but if you want, I'll ___ try ___ to love a-gain. Ba - by, I'll try ___
and if you want, I'll ___ try ___ to love a-gain. Ba - by, I'll try ___

___ to love a - gain, but I know: ___ }
___ to love a - gain, but I know: ___ }

The first cut is the deep -

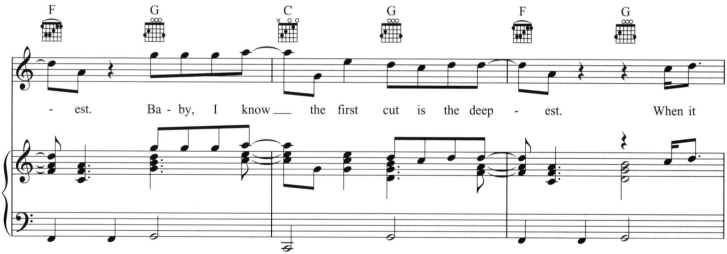

- est. Ba - by, I know ___ the first cut is the deep - est. When it

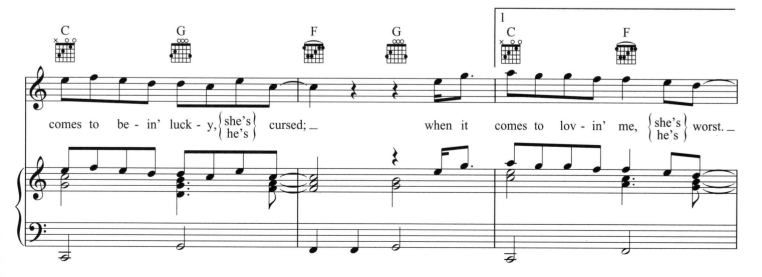

comes to be - in' luck - y, {she's / he's} cursed; ___ when it comes to lov - in' me, {she's / he's} worst. ___

I still

comes to lov - in' me, {she's he's} worst. ___

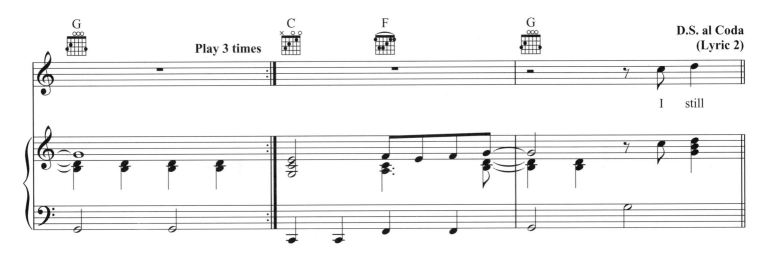

Play 3 times

D.S. al Coda (Lyric 2)

I still

CODA

___ to love a - gain but I know: ___

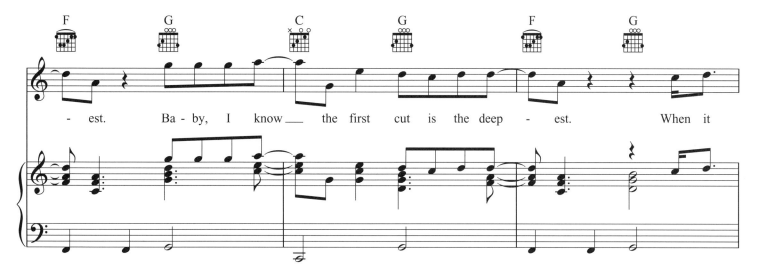

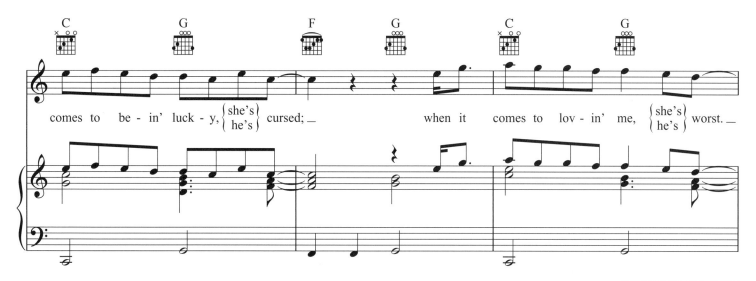

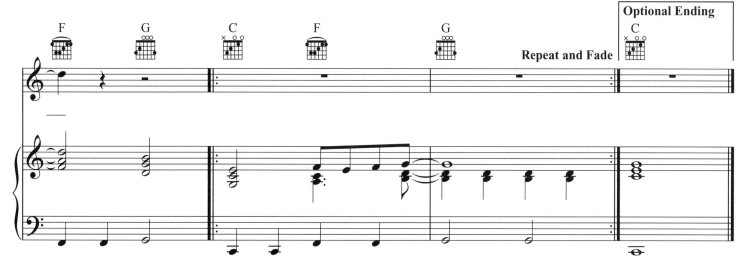

FLY LIKE AN EAGLE

Words and Music by
STEVE MILLER

Tick, tock,— tick. Doot, doot, do, do.

Time keeps on slip-pin', slip-pin', slip-pin' _____ in-to the fu-

-ture. _____

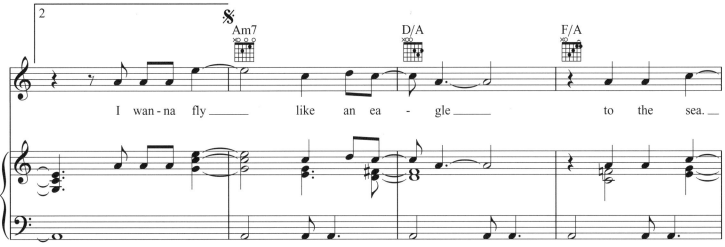

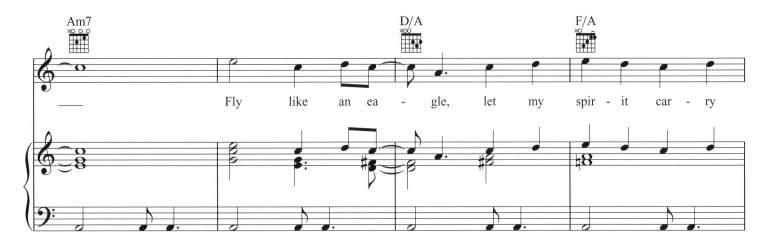

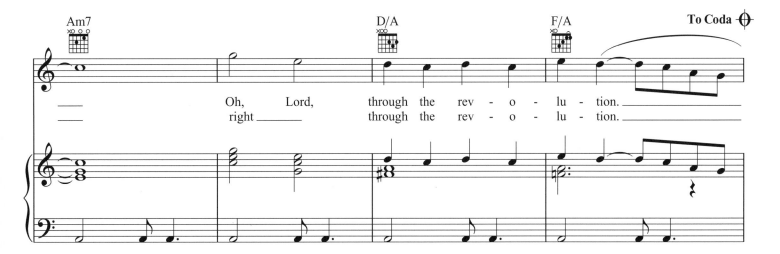

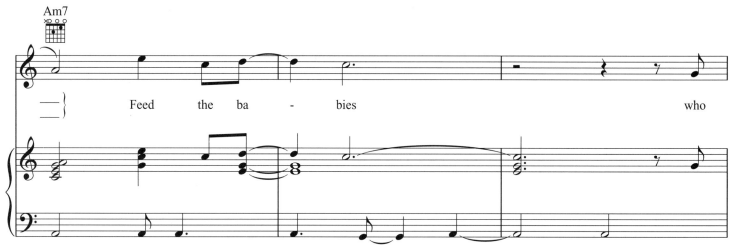

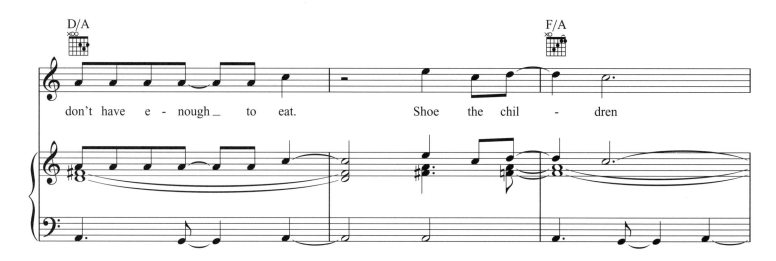

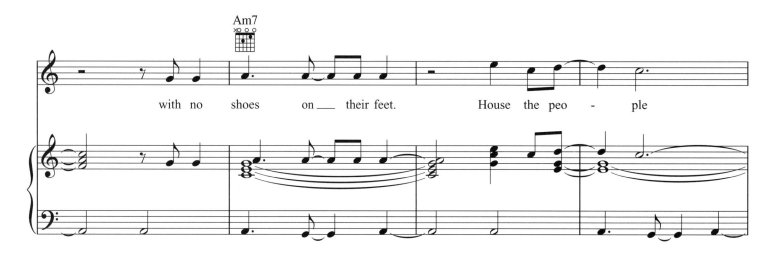

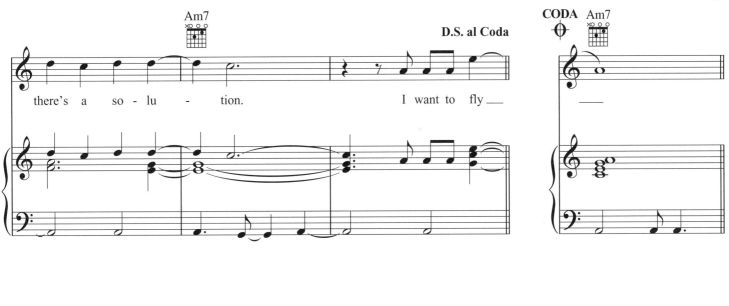

there's a so-lu-tion.   I want to fly

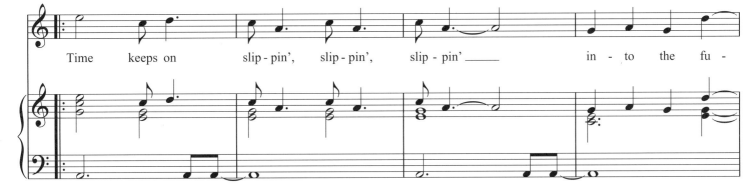

Time keeps on slip-pin', slip-pin', slip-pin' _____ in-to the fu-

-ture.

Play 4 times

Do, doot - n' do do.   Do, doot - n' do do.

I want to fly like an ea - gle _____

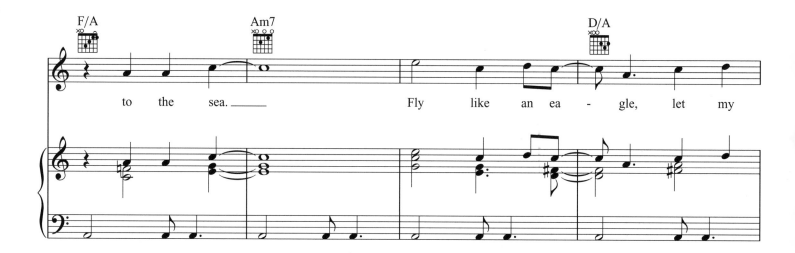

to the sea. _____ Fly like an ea - gle, let my

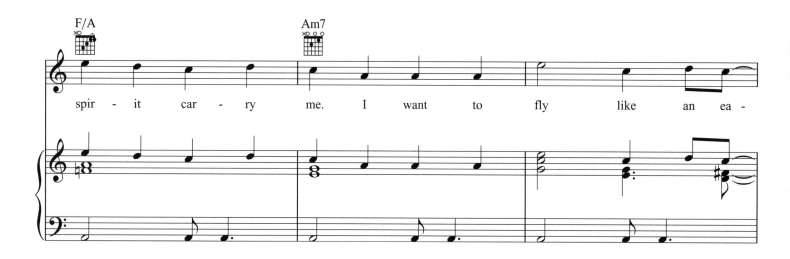

spir - it car - ry me. I want to fly like an ea -

- gle _____ till I'm free, _____

FOLSOM PRISON BLUES

Words and Music by
JOHN R. CASH

1. I hear the train a-com-in', it's roll-in' 'round the
2. I was just a ba-by, my ma-ma told me,
3.,4. (*See additional lyrics*)

bend, And I ain't seen the sun-shine since I don't know
"Son, _____ al-ways be a good boy; don't ev-er play with

when. I'm stuck at Fol-som Pris-on and time keeps
guns." But I shot a man in Re-no just _____ to

drag - gin' on. ___
watch him die. ___

But that train keeps roll - in' on down to
When I hear that whis - tle blow - in', I hang my

San An - tone. ___
head and cry. ___

When I
Well,

Additional Lyrics

3. I bet there's rich folks eatin' in a fancy dining car;
   They're prob'ly drinkin' coffee and smokin' big cigars.
   But I know I had it comin', I know I can't be free,
   But those people keep a-movin', and that's what tortures me.

4. Well, if they freed me from this prison, if that railroad train was mine,
   I bet I'd move on over a little farther down the line.
   Far from Folsom Prison, that's where I want to stay,
   And I'd let that lonesome whistle blow my blues away.

FREE FALLIN'

Words and Music by TOM PETTY
and JEFF LYNNE

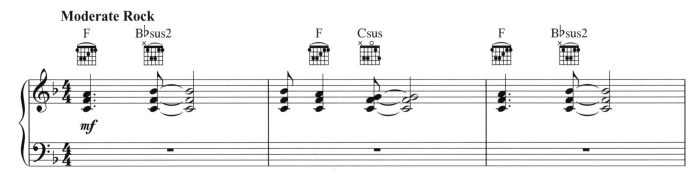

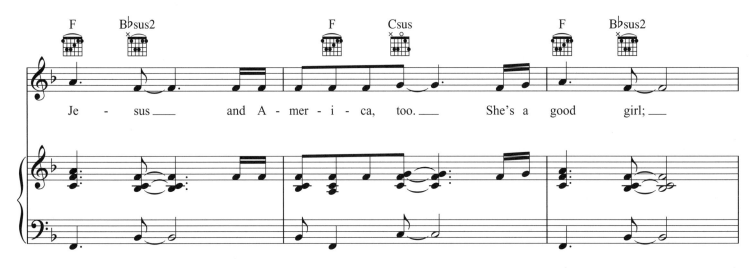

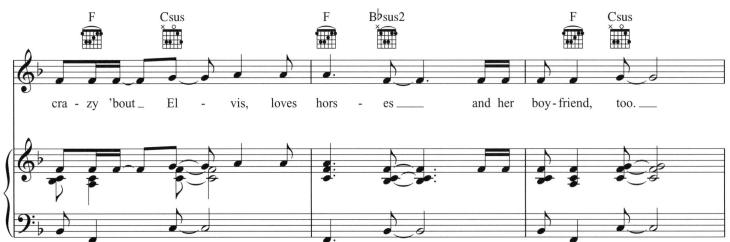

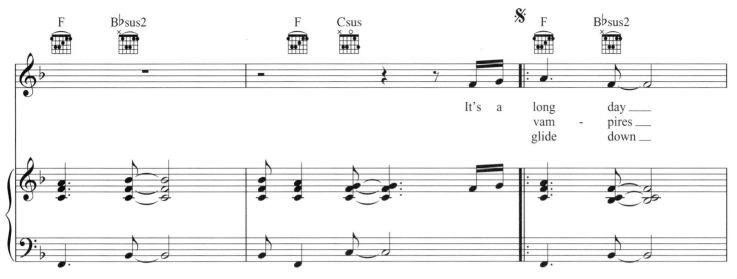

It's a   long   day ___
vam - pires ___
glide   down ___

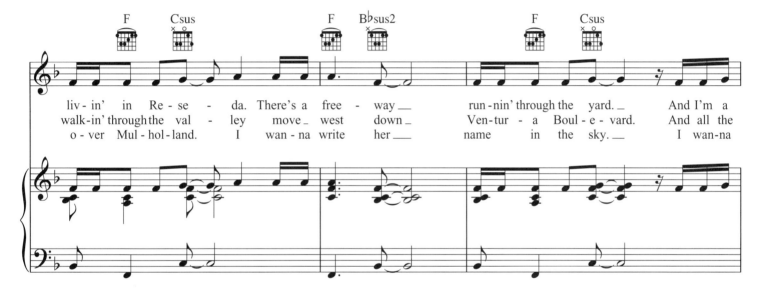

liv - in' in Re - se - da. There's a free - way ___ run - nin' through the yard. __ And I'm a
walk - in' through the val - ley move _ west down _ Ven - tur - a Boul - e - vard. And all the
o - ver Mul - hol - land. I wan - na write her __ name in the sky. __ I wan - na

bad   boy __ 'cause I don't e - ven miss __ her. I'm a bad   boy __ for
bad   boys __ are stand - ing in the shad - ows. And the good girls __ are
free   fall __ out in - to noth - in'. Gon - na leave this __

break-in' her __ heart. __
home with bro-ken hearts. __ } And I'm free, free

world for a while. __ }

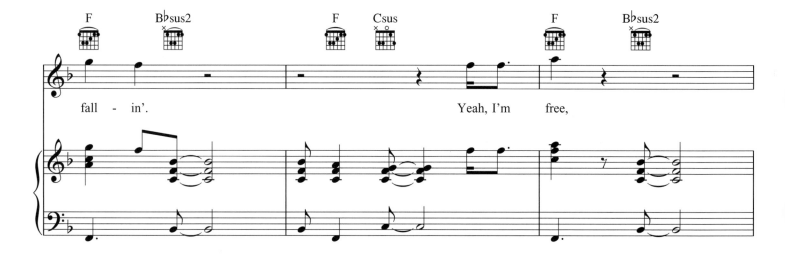

fall - in'. Yeah, I'm free,

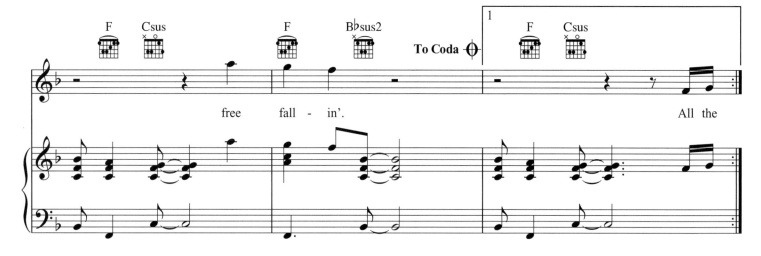

To Coda ⊕

free fall - in'. All the

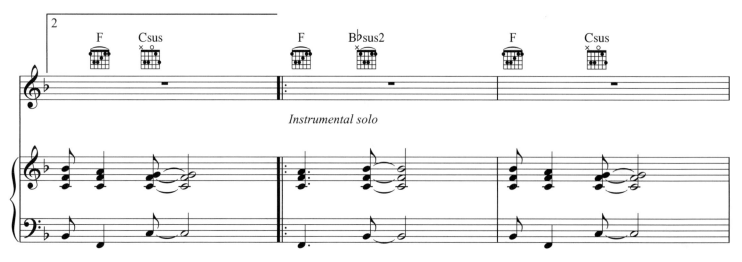

Instrumental solo

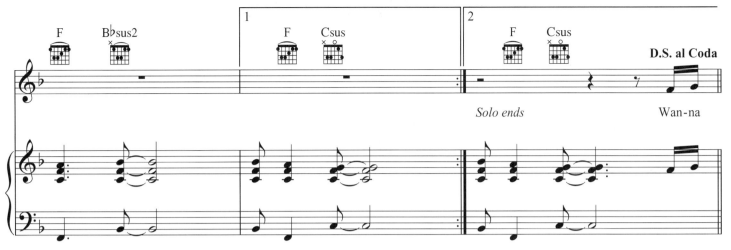

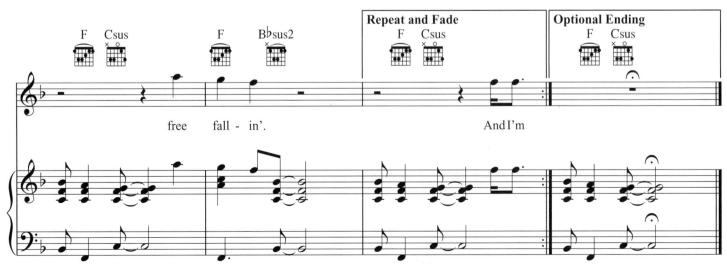

HOUND DOG

Words and Music by JERRY LEIBER
and MIKE STOLLER

nev - er caught a rab - bit and you ain't no friend of mine. __

You ain't noth - in' but a
You ain't noth - in' but a

D.S. al Coda

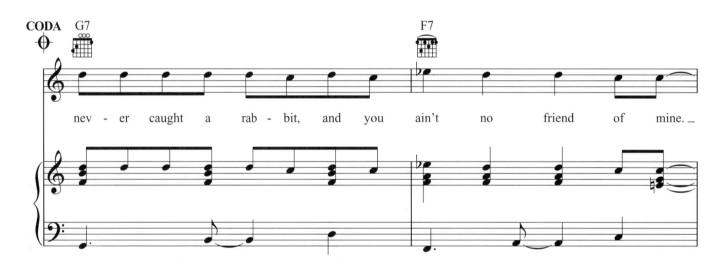

CODA

nev - er caught a rab - bit, and you ain't no friend of mine. __

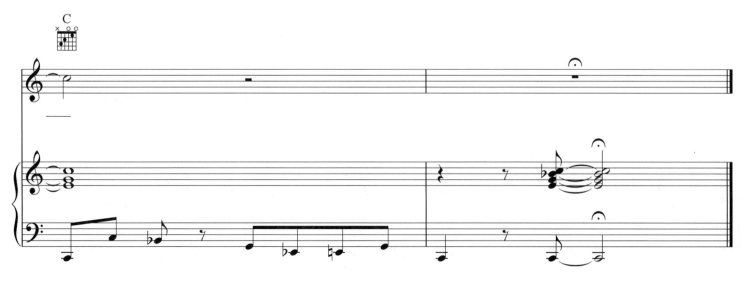

GET BACK

Words and Music by JOHN LENNON
and PAUL McCARTNEY

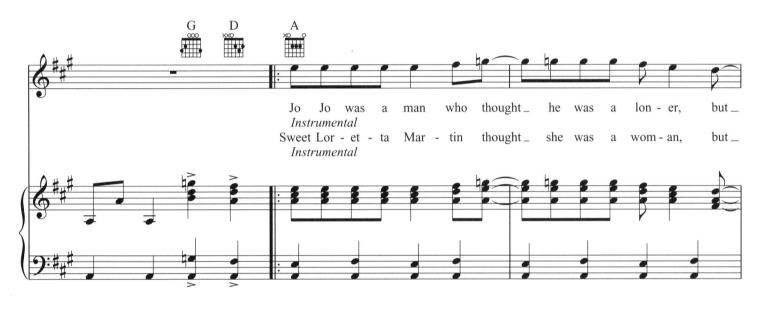

Jo Jo was a man who thought _ he was a lon - er, but _
Instrumental
Sweet Lor - et - ta Mar - tin thought _ she was a wom - an, but _
Instrumental

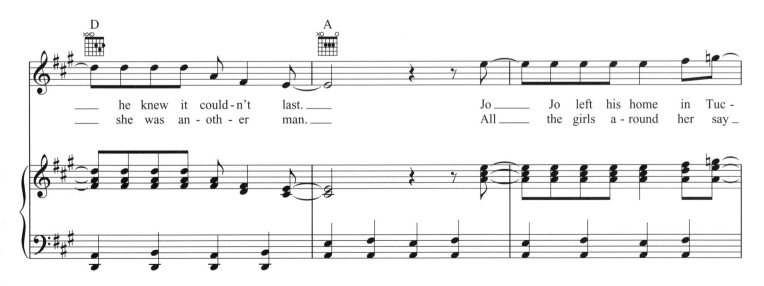

_ he knew it could - n't last. _
_ she was an - oth - er man. _
Jo _ Jo left his home in Tuc -
All _ the girls a - round her say _

(Get back, Jo Jo)

Spoken ad lib:

Get back, Loretta, your momma's waitin' for you
Wearin' her high heel shoes and a low neck sweater.
Get back home, Loretta.

Repeat and Fade

I FOUGHT THE LAW

Words and Music by
SONNY CURTIS

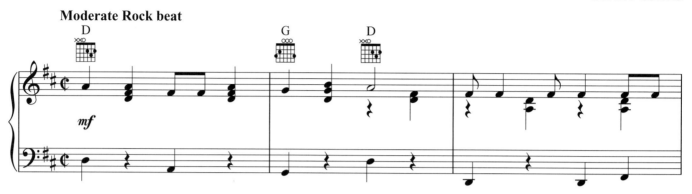

Moderate Rock beat

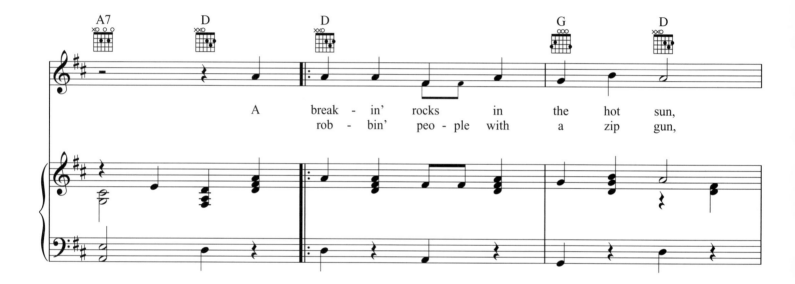

A break-in' rocks in the hot sun,
rob-in' peo-ple with a zip gun,

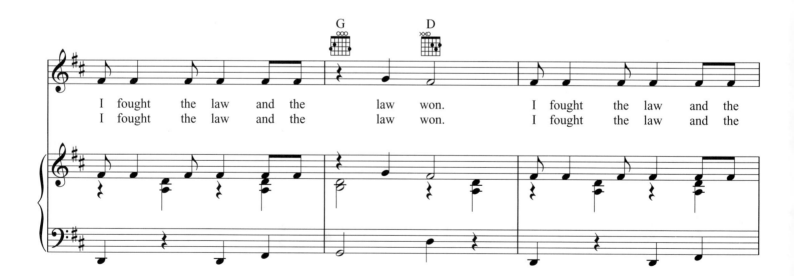

I fought the law and the law won. I fought the law and the
I fought the law and the law won. I fought the law and the

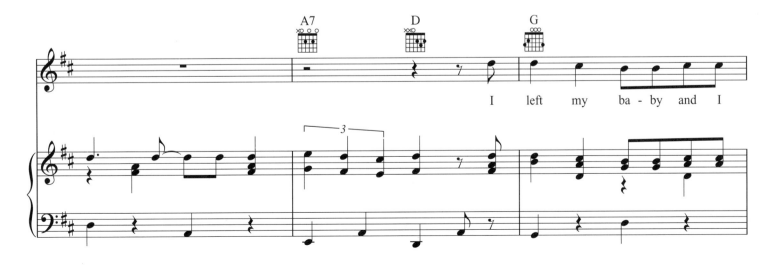

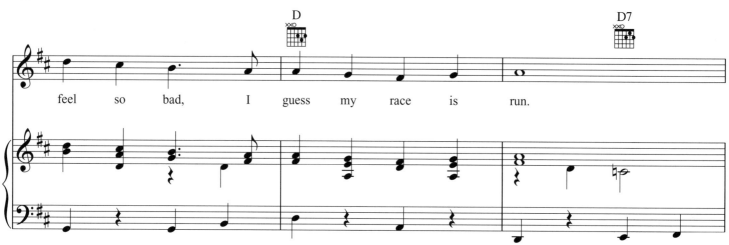

feel so bad, I guess my race is run.

She's the best girl I've ev - er had, I fought the law and the

law won. I fought the law and the law won.

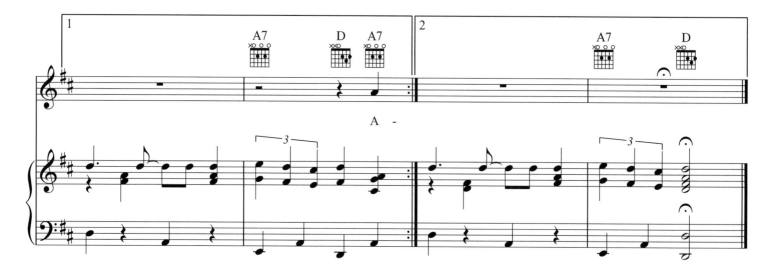

A -

HOLD MY HAND

Words and Music by DARIUS CARLOS RUCKER,
EVERETT DEAN FELBER, MARK WILLIAM BRYAN
and JAMES GEORGE SONEFELD

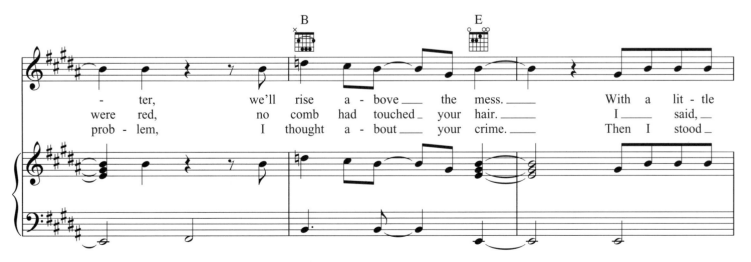

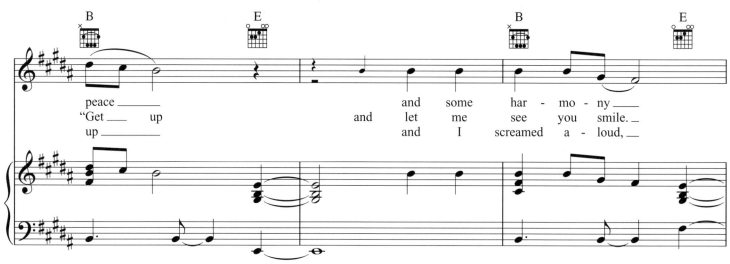

peace _____ and some har - mo - ny _____
"Get ___ up and let me see you smile. __
up _____ and I screamed a - loud, __

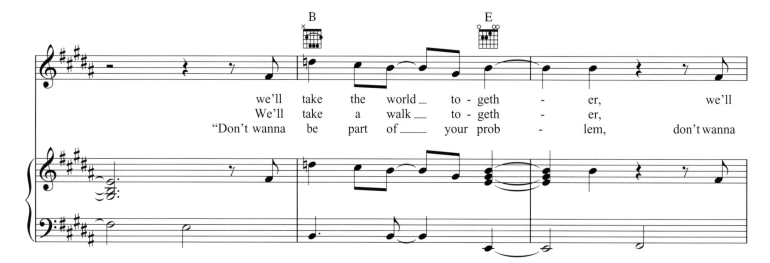

we'll take the world _ to - geth - er, we'll
We'll take a walk _ to - geth - er, we'll
"Don't wanna be part of ____ your prob - lem, don't wanna

take 'em by ___ the hand. _____
walk the road ___ a while." _____
be part of ____ your crowd." _____
'Cause I got a

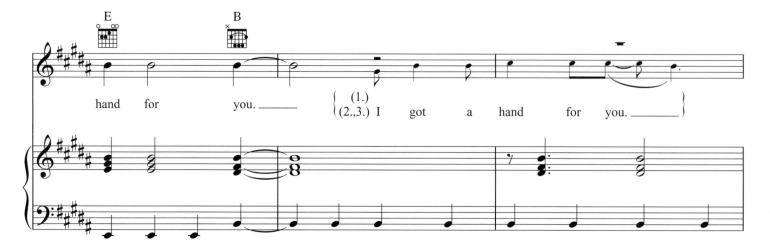

hand for you. _____
(1.)
(2.,3.) I got a hand for you. _____

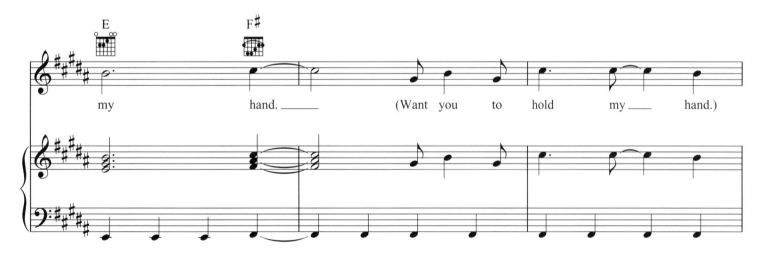

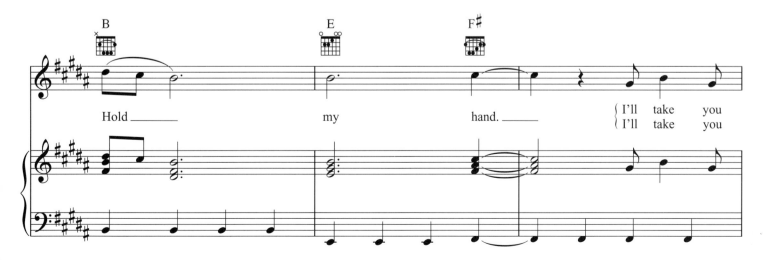

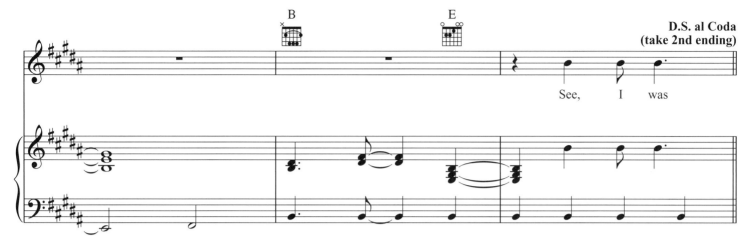

D.S. al Coda
(take 2nd ending)

See, I was

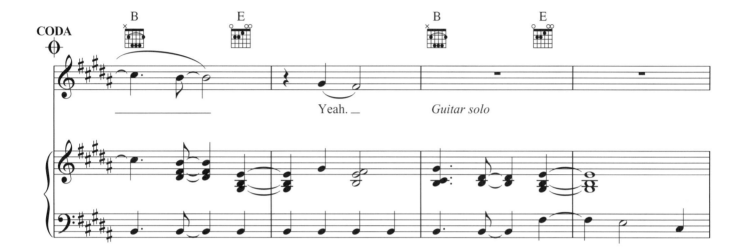

CODA

_____ Yeah. __ *Guitar solo*

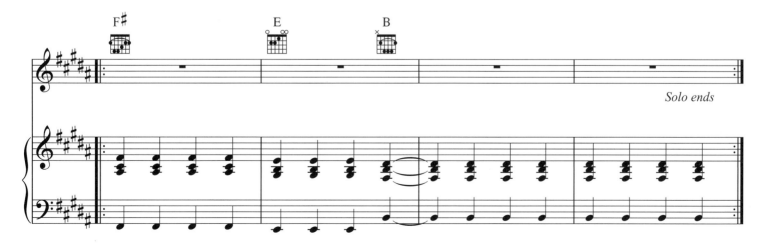

Solo ends

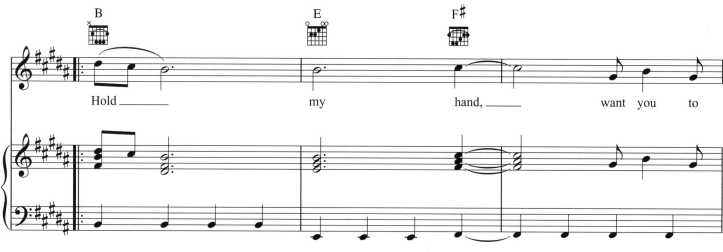

oh, _____ no, no, no. I wan - na

love you _____ the best that, the best that I can, _____

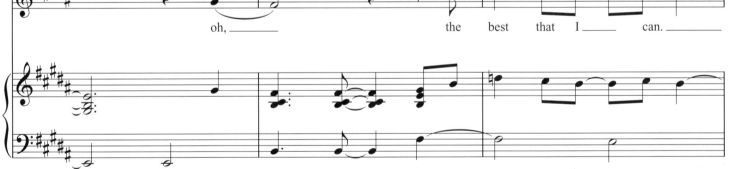

oh, _____ the best that I _____ can. _____

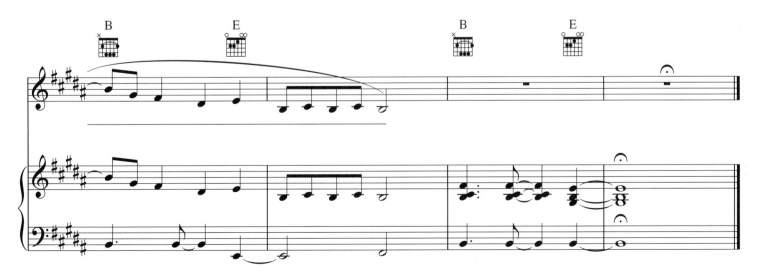

IF I WERE A CARPENTER

Words and Music by
TIM HARDIN

If I ___ were a car - pen - ter, ___
If I ___ worked my hands in wood, ___

and you were a la - dy,   would you mar - ry me
would you still ___ love me?   An - swer me, ___ babe,

Save my love thru lone - li - ness, ___ save my love for sor - row, I've giv - en you my on - li - ness, ___ come and give me your to - mor - row. ___

I HAVE A DREAM

Words and Music by BENNY ANDERSSON
and BJÖRN ULVAEUS

of a fair - y tale, you can take the fu - ture

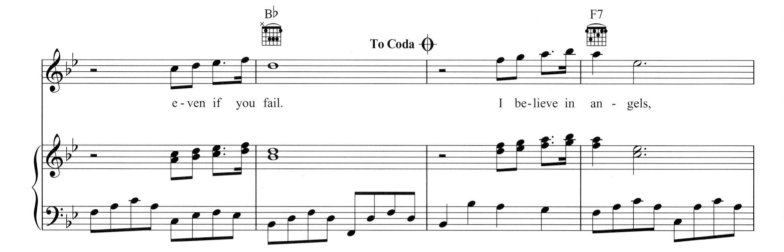

e - ven if you fail. I be-lieve in an - gels,

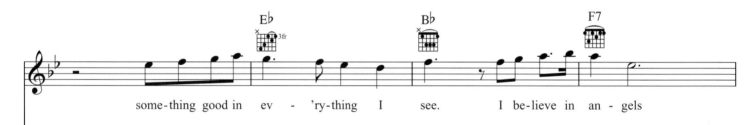

some-thing good in ev - 'ry-thing I see. I be-lieve in an - gels

when I know the time is right for me, I'll cross the stream,

I have a dream. I have a dream,

a fan - ta - sy, to help me through _____

re - al - i - ty. And my des - ti - na - tion

makes it worth the while, push-ing through the dark - ness

still an-oth-er mile.   I be-lieve _____ in

an - gels,   some-thing good in ev - 'ry-thing I see.   I be-lieve in

an - gels   when I know the time   is right for

me, I'll cross   the stream,   I have   a dream.

I'll cross the stream, I have a dream.

D.S. al Coda

I have a

CODA

I be-lieve _____ in an - gels,

some-thing good in ev - 'ry-thing I see. I be-lieve in

an - gels when I know the time is right for

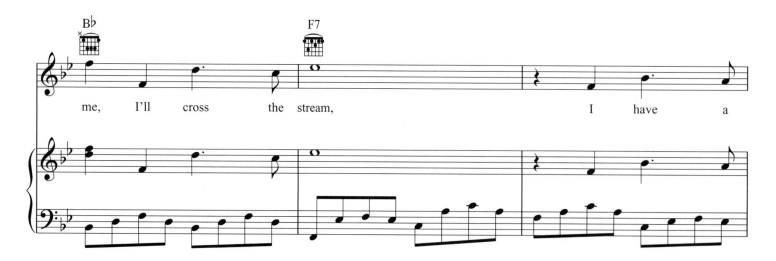

me, I'll cross the stream, I have a

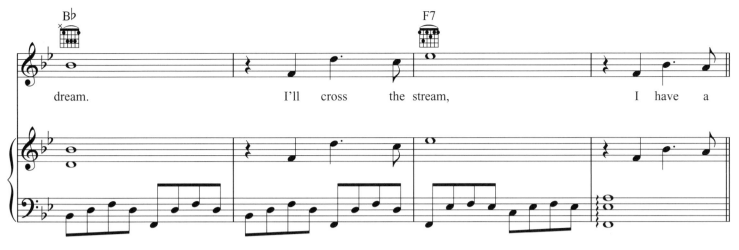

dream.   I'll   cross   the   stream,   I have a

dream. Na   na   na   na   na   na   na   na   na   na   na   na   na   na   na   na   na   na   na

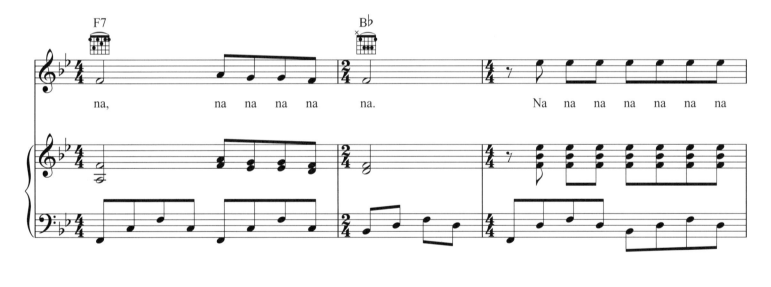

na,   na   na   na   na   na.   Na   na   na   na   na   na   na

Repeat and Fade

na na na na na na na na   na na na na   na,   na na na na   na,   na na na na,

I'LL TAKE YOU THERE

Words and Music by
ALVERTIS ISBELL

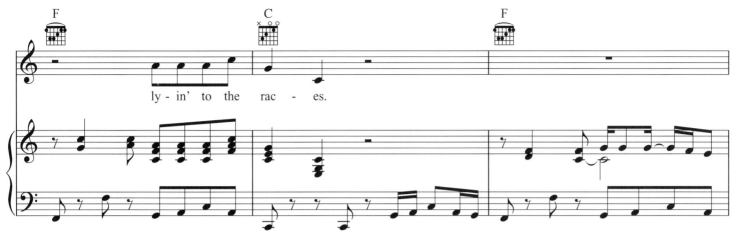

ly - in' to the rac - es.

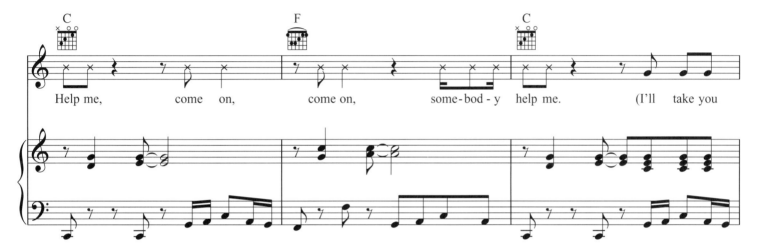

Help me, come on, come on, some-bod - y help me. (I'll take you

there.) Help me, y'all. (I'll take you there.)

Help me now. (I'll take you there.) (I'll take you

there.) Mer- cy. (I'll take you there.)

Let me take you there. (I'll take you there.) Let me take you. (I'll take you

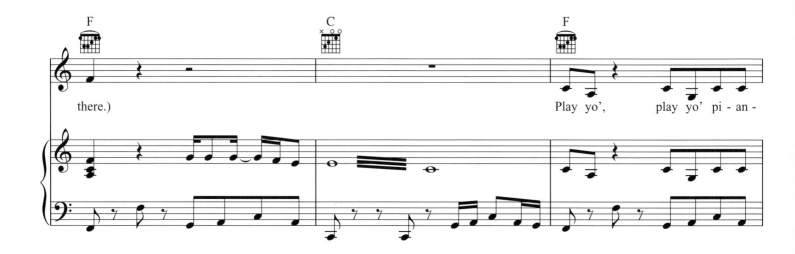

there.) Play yo', play yo' pi - an -

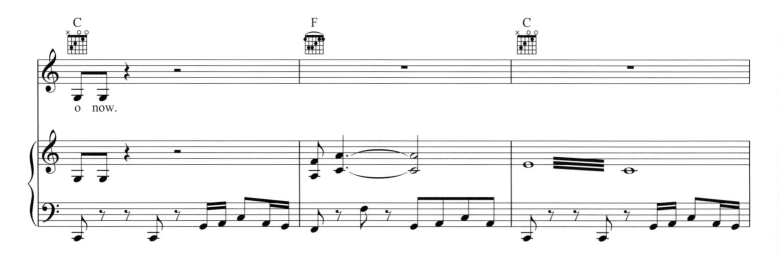

o now.

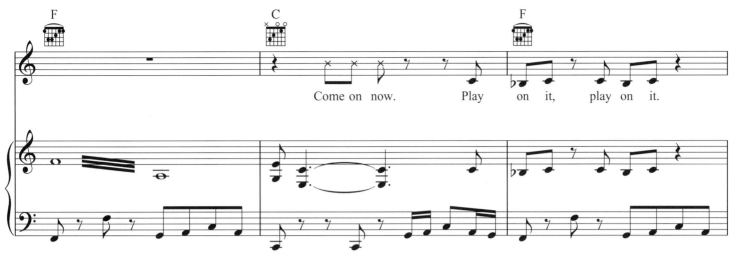

Come on now. Play on it, play on it.

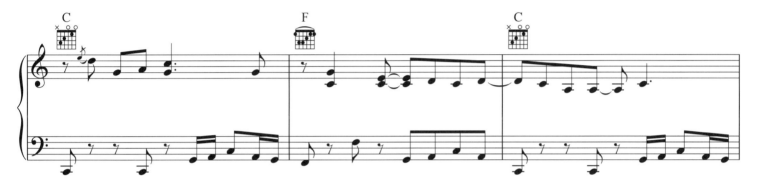

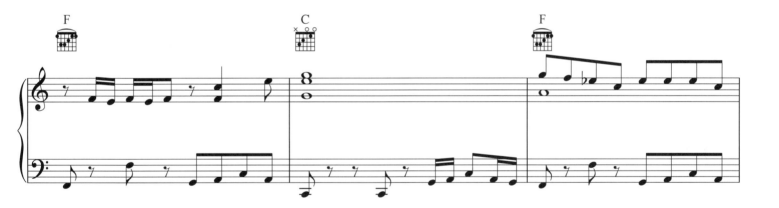

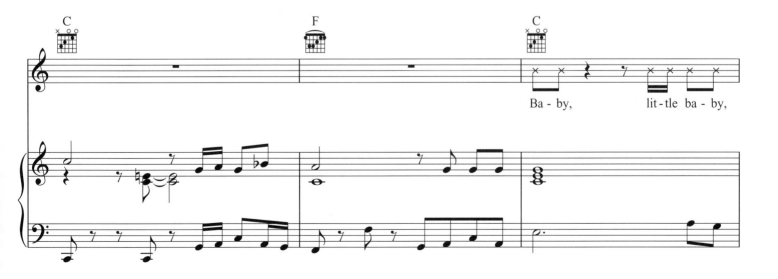

Ba - by, lit - tle ba - by,

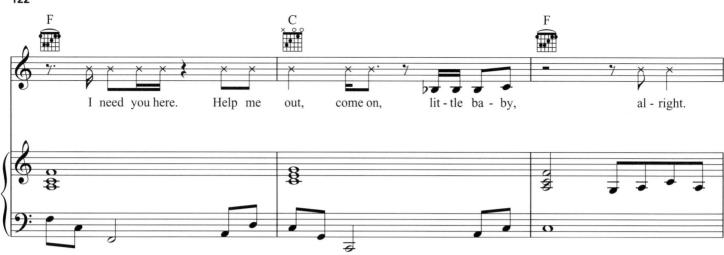

I need you here. Help me out, come on, lit-tle ba-by, al-right.

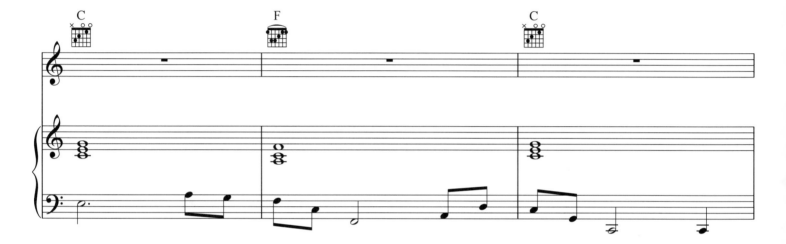

I, oh, I, I know a

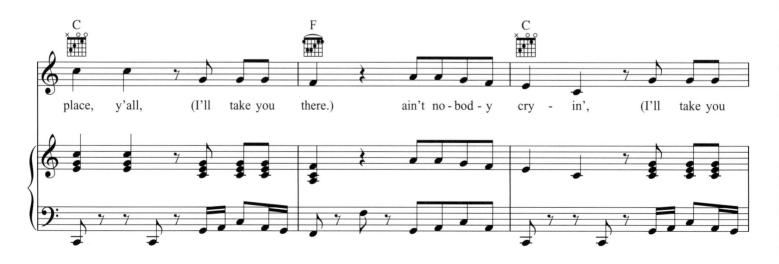

place, y'all, (I'll take you there.) ain't no-bod-y cry-in', (I'll take you

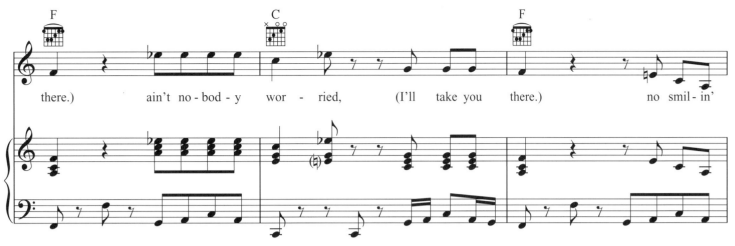

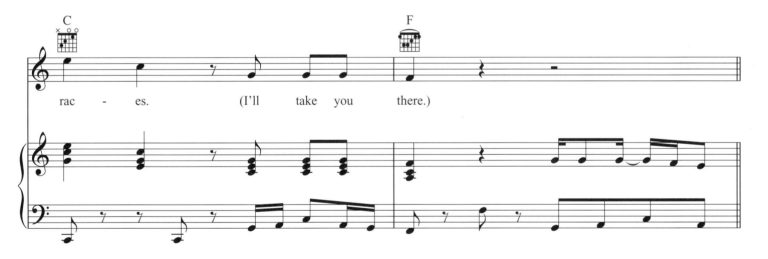

THE JOKER

Words and Music by STEVE MILLER,
EDDIE CURTIS and AHMET ERTEGUN

speak of the pom-pa-tus of love.

Peo-ple talk ___ a-bout ___ me, ba - by, ___

say I'm do - ing you wrong, ___ do - ing you wrong. ___

Well, don't you wor - ry, ba - by, don't wor - ry 'cause I'm

right here, right here, right here, right there at home. ___ 'Cause I'm a

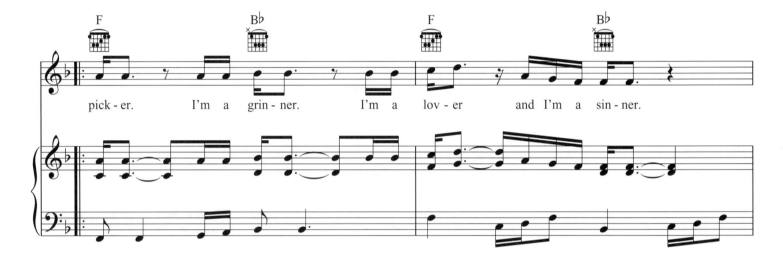

pick - er. I'm a grin - ner. I'm a lov - er and I'm a sin - ner.

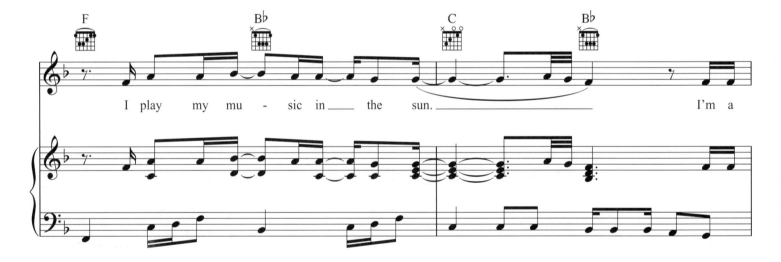

I play my mu - sic in ___ the sun. ___ I'm a

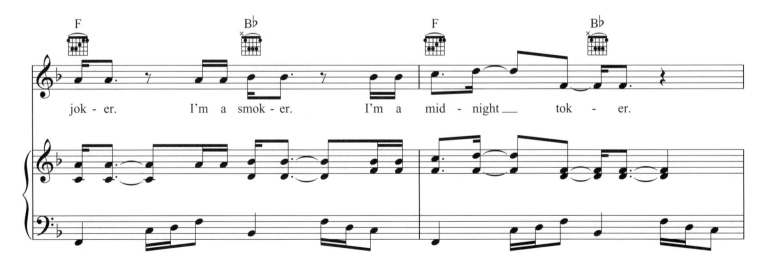

jok - er. I'm a smok - er. I'm a mid - night ___ tok - er.

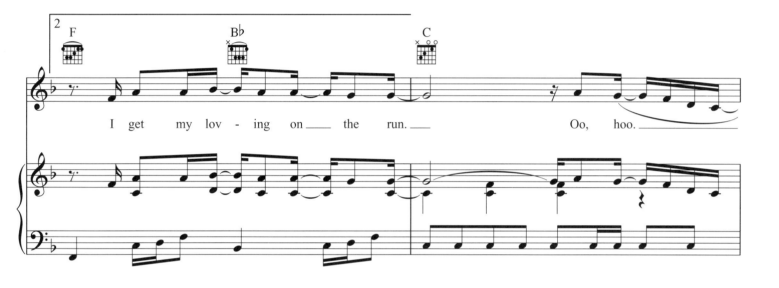

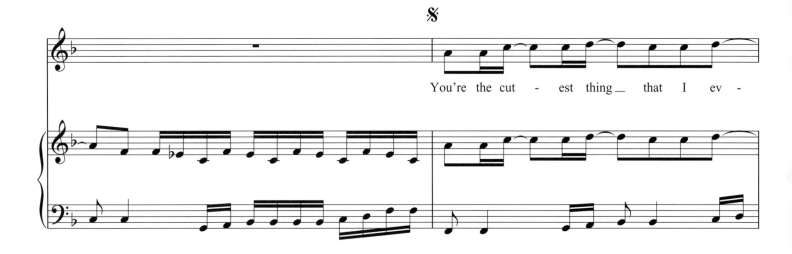

You're the cut - est thing__ that I ev -

- er did see._____ I real - ly love__ your peach - es, wan - na

shake your tree.____ Lov-ey dov - ey, lov-ey dov-ey, lov-ey

To Coda ⊕

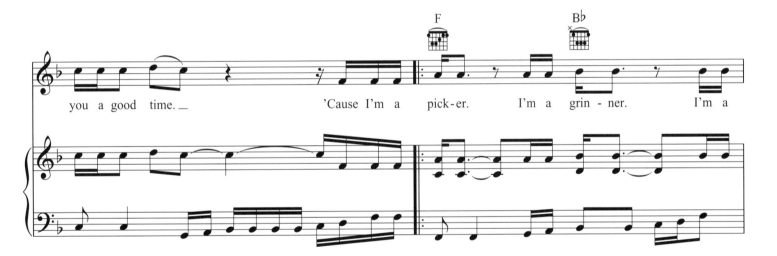

dov-ey all the time._____ Oo, wee, ba - by, I'll sure show

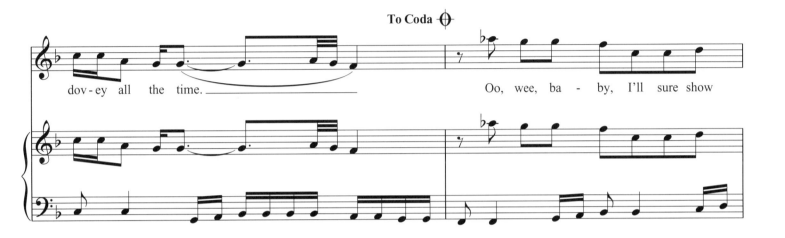

you a good time.__ 'Cause I'm a pick-er. I'm a grin - ner. I'm a

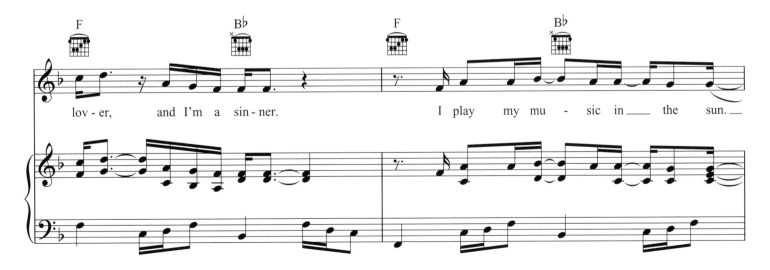

lov - er, and I'm a sin-ner. I play my mu - sic in__ the sun.__

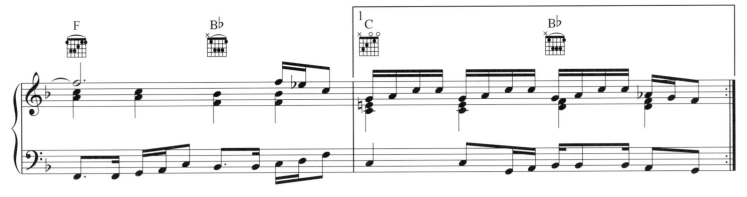

Oo, hoo. ____ Oo, hoo. ____

Peo - ple keep talk - in' a - bout ___ me, ba - by.

They say I'm do - ing you wrong. ____

Well, don't you wor-ry. Don't wor - ry. No, don't wor - ry, ma - ma,

D.S. al Coda

'cause I'm right here at home.

CODA

Come on, babe, ___ and I'll show you a good time. ___

Repeat and Fade **Optional Ending**

JOLENE

Words and Music by
DOLLY PARTON

Jo - lene, Jo - lene, Jo - lene, Jo -
lene, _____ I'm beg-ging of you, please don't take my man. _____
Jo - lene, Jo - lene, Jo - lene, Jo -

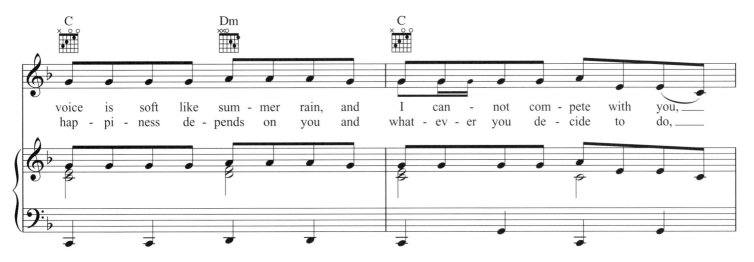

voice is soft like sum - mer rain, and I can - not com - pete with you, ___
hap - pi - ness de - pends on you and what - ev - er you de - cide to do, ___

To Coda ⊕

Jo - lene. He
Jo - lene. Jo -

talks a - bout you in his sleep and there's noth - ing I can do to keep from

cry - in' when he calls your name, Jo - lene. ___ And

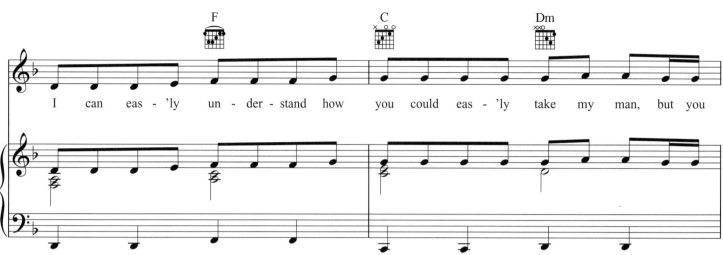

I can eas-'ly un-der-stand how you could eas-'ly take my man, but you

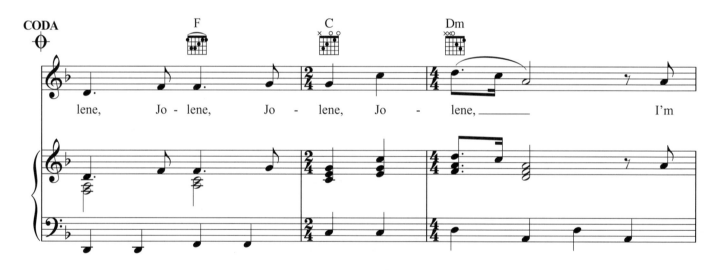

D.S. al Coda

don't know what he means to me, Jo - lene.

Jo -

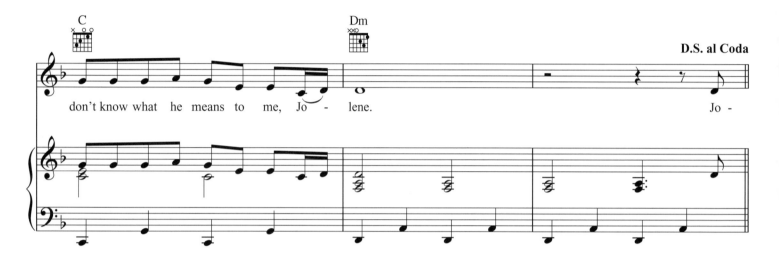

CODA

lene, Jo - lene, Jo - lene, Jo - lene, _____

I'm

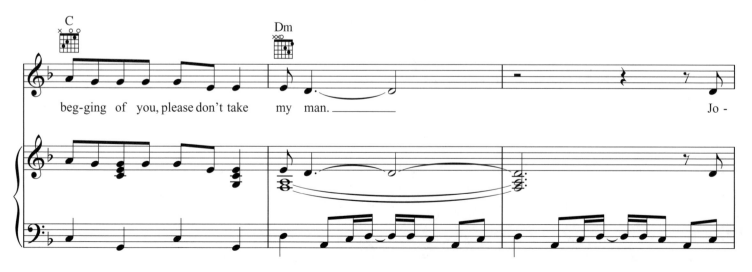

beg-ging of you, please don't take my man. _____

Jo -

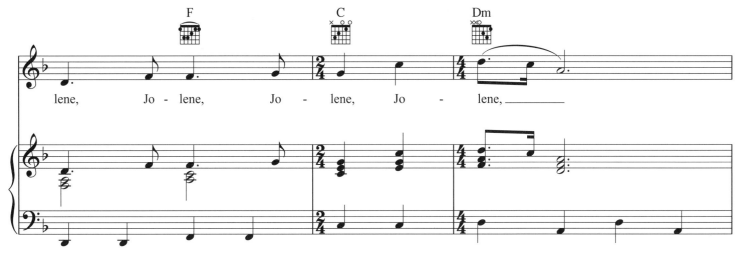

lene,   Jo - lene,   Jo - lene,   Jo - lene, _____

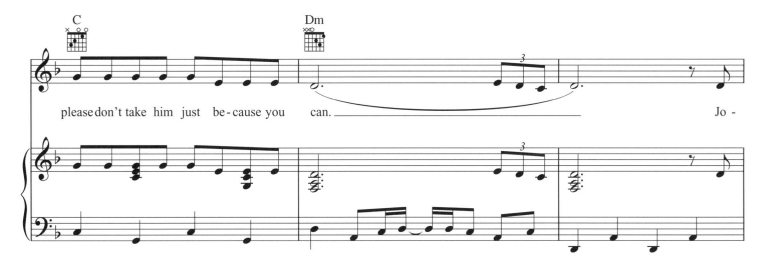

please don't take him just be-cause you can. _____   Jo -

lene,   Jo - lene,   please don't take my man, Jo - lene,   Jo -

lene,   Jo - lene.   My hap - pi - ness de-pends on you, Jo - lene.

JUST THE WAY YOU ARE

Words and Music by BRUNO MARS,
ARI LEVINE, PHILIP LAWRENCE,
KHARI CAIN and KHALIL WALTON

Moderate Hip-Hop groove

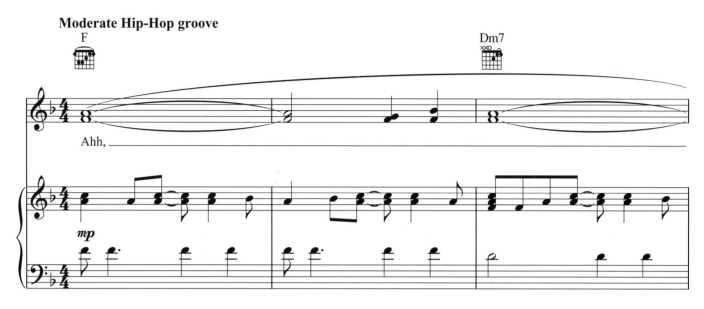

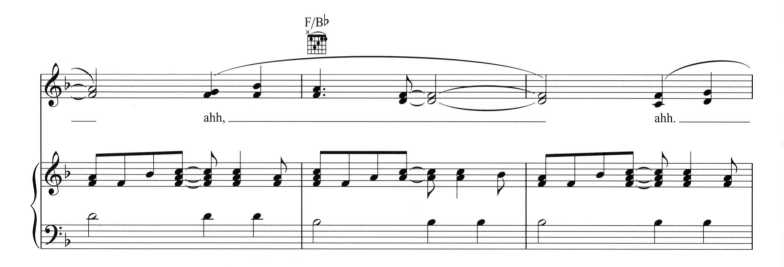

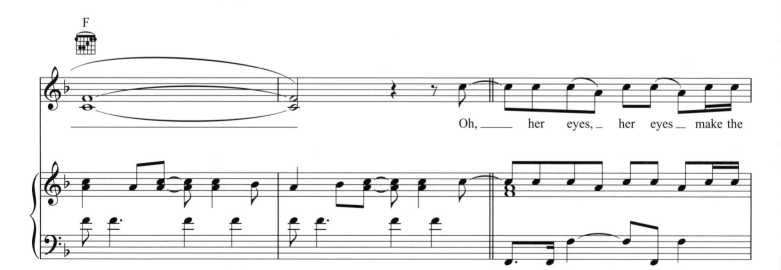

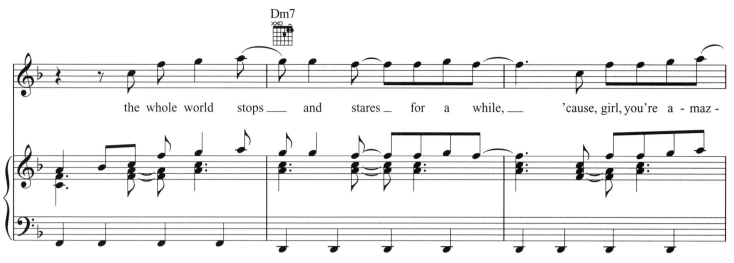

the whole world stops ___ and stares ___ for a while, ___ 'cause, girl, you're a - maz-

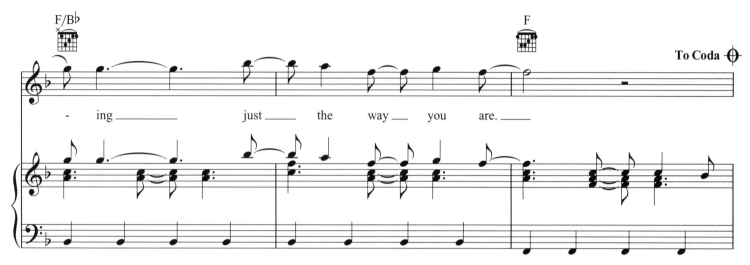

- ing ___ just ___ the way ___ you are. ___

To Coda ⊕

Yeah. ___ Her lips, ___ her lips, ___ I could kiss them all ___ day if ___ she'd let me.

Her laugh, ___ her laugh, ___ she hates but I ___ think it's ___ so sex - y. She's so beau - ti - ful, ___

CODA

The way _ you _ are, _ the way _ you _ are. _

Dm7 **F/B♭**

Girl, you're a - maz - ing _ just _

F

_ the way _ you _ are. _ When I see your face, _

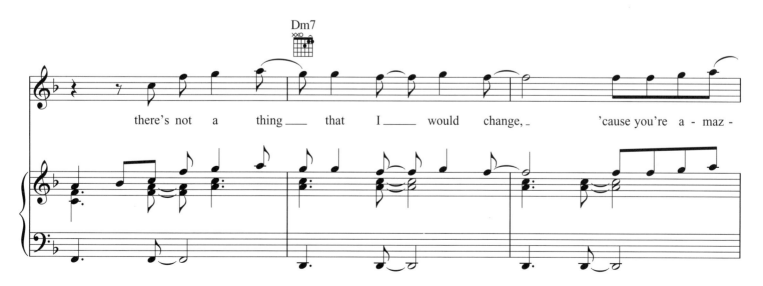

Dm7

there's not a thing _ that I _ would change, _ 'cause you're a - maz -

JUST MY IMAGINATION
(Running Away with Me)

Words and Music by NORMAN J. WHITFIELD
and BARRETT STRONG

I tell you, To have a girl like her _____ is tru - ly
I _____ can vis-ual-

a dream come _ true. _____ Out of all the fel-lows in the
ize _ it _ all. _____ This could-n't be a dream, far too

world, she be-longs _ to you." _____ But it was
real it all seems. _ But it was

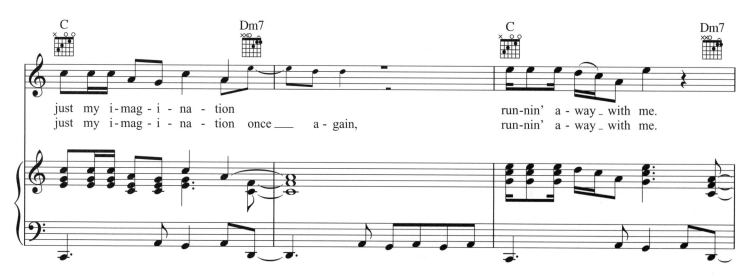

just my i-mag-i-na-tion run-nin' a-way _ with me.
just my i-mag-i-na-tion once _ a-gain, run-nin' a-way _ with me.

Don't ev - er let an - oth - er take her love from me, or I would

sure - ly die." _____ Her love is heav - en - ly.

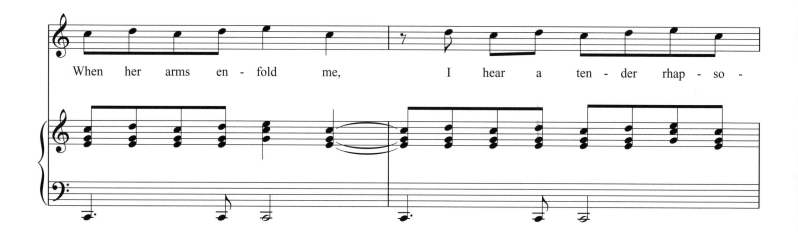

When her arms en - fold me, I hear a ten - der rhap - so -

dy. But in re - al - i - ty, she does - n't e - ven know me. __

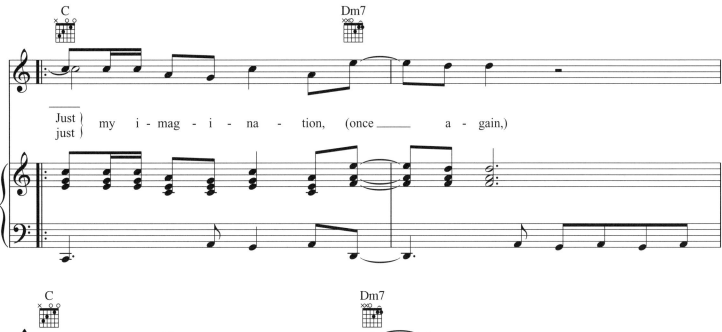

Just / just my i-mag-i-na-tion, (once ___ a-gain,)

run-nin' a-way ___ with me. Oh, ___ tell you, it was

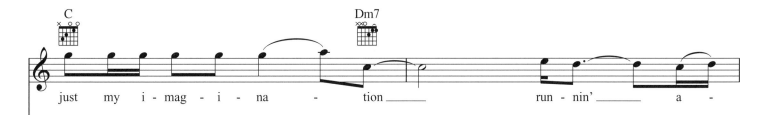

just my i-mag-i-na - tion ___ run-nin' ___ a-

Repeat and Fade

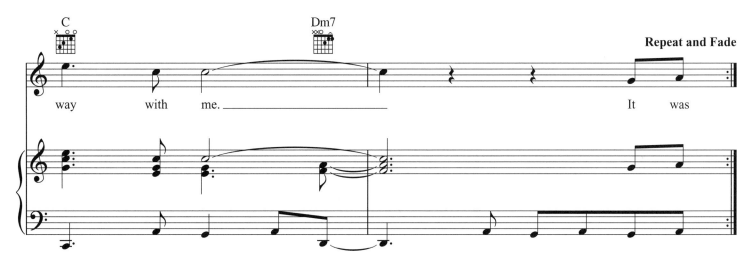

way with me. ___ It was

LA BAMBA

By RICHARD VALENZUELA

Moderate Latin Rock beat

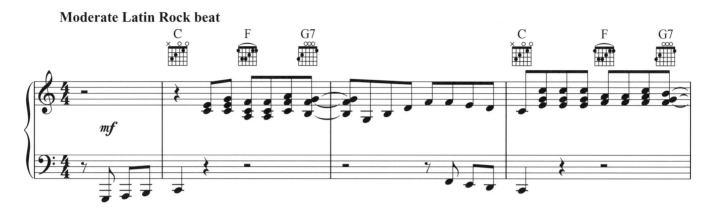

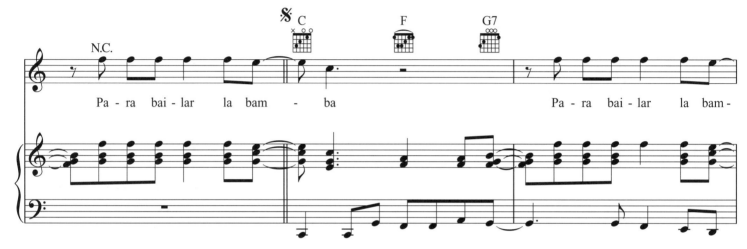

Pa - ra bai - lar la bam - ba   Pa - ra bai - lar la bam-

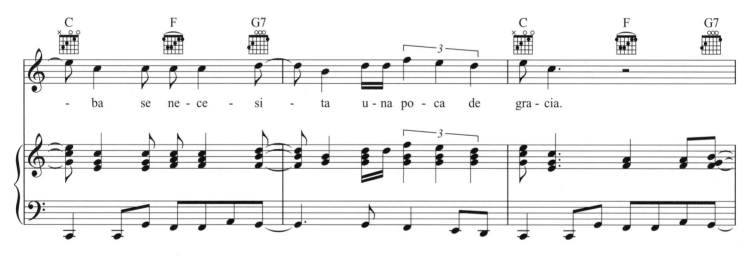

-ba se ne - ce - si - ta u - na po - ca de gra - cia.

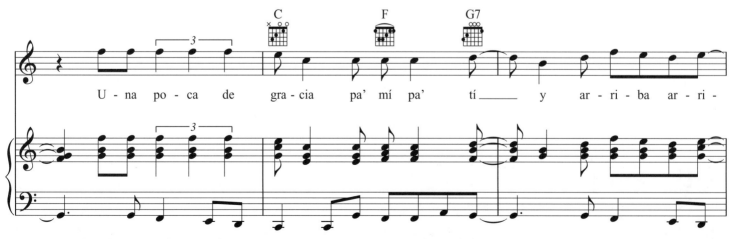

U - na po - ca de gra - cia pa' mí pa' tí___ y ar - ri - ba ar - ri-

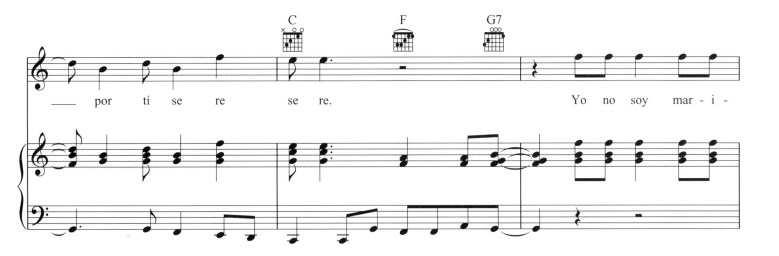

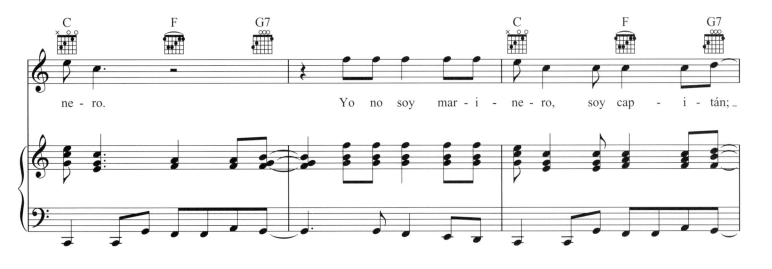

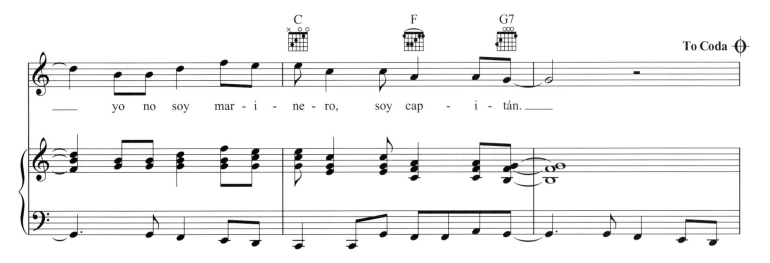

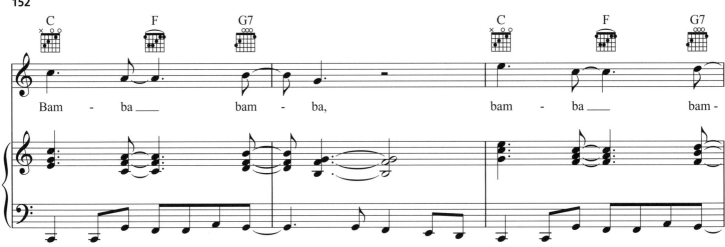

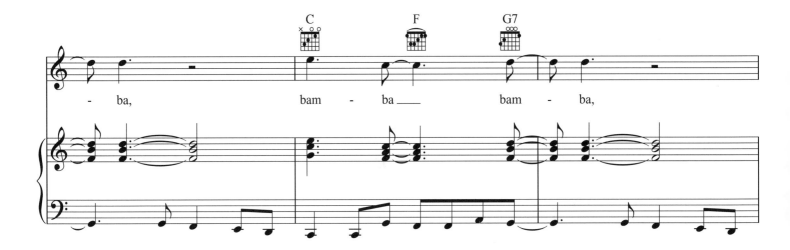

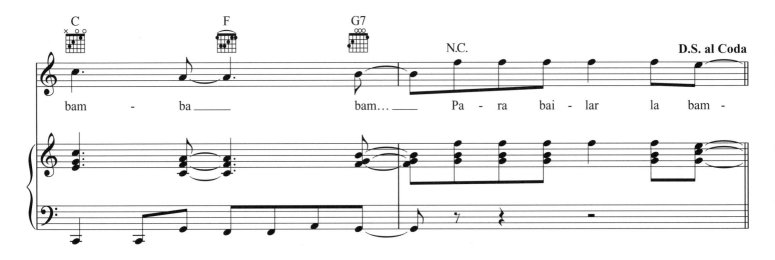

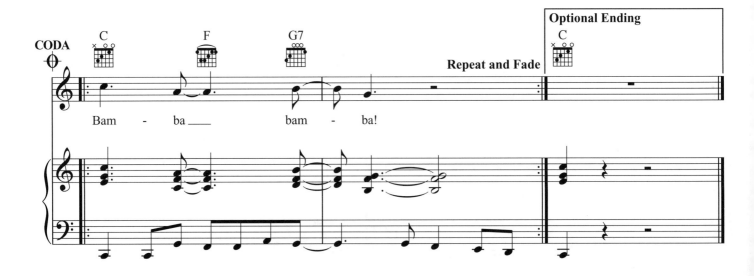

KEEP YOUR HANDS TO YOURSELF

Words and Music by
DANIEL BAIRD

Blues Rock

I got a lit-tle change in my pock-et go-ing jin - gle - in - gle - in - gle, want to call ___

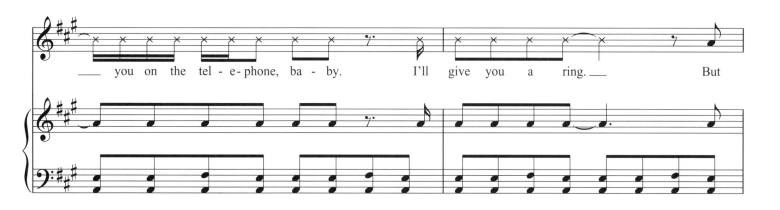

___ you on the tel - e - phone, ba - by. I'll give you a ring. ___ But

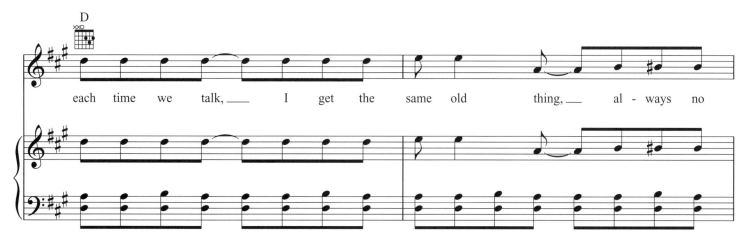

each time we talk, ___ I get the same old thing, ___ al - ways no

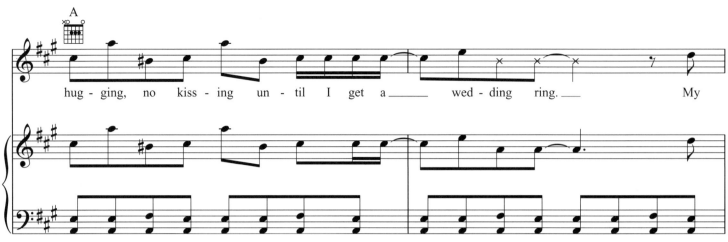

hug-ging, no kiss-ing un-til I get a_____ wed-ding ring.___ My

hon-ey, my___ ba-by,___ don't put my love up-on no shelf.___ She said, "Don't

give me no___ lines,___ and keep your hands to your-self."___

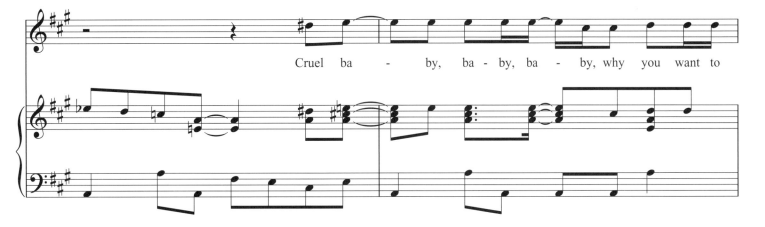

Cruel ba - by, ba - by, ba - by, why you want to

treat me this way?___ You know I'm still your lov - er boy,___ I still

D

feel the same ___ way. That's when she told ___ me a sto - ry 'bout free

A

milk and a cow,___ and said no hug - ging, no kiss - ing un - til I get a

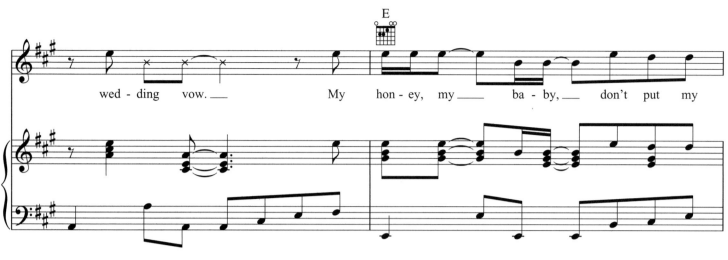

wed - ding vow. ___ My hon - ey, my ___ ba - by, ___ don't put my

love up - on no shelf. ___ She said, "Don't hand me no ___ lines, ___ and keep your

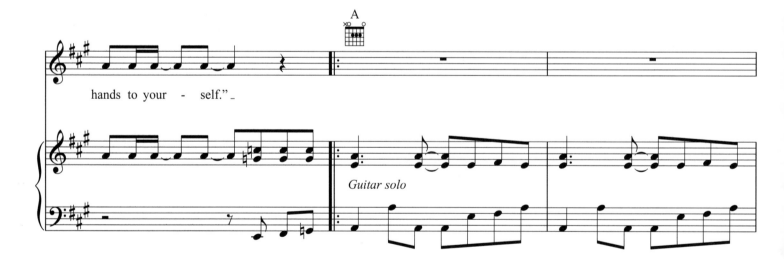

hands to your - self." ___

Guitar solo

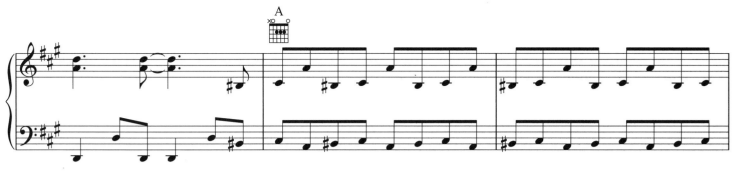

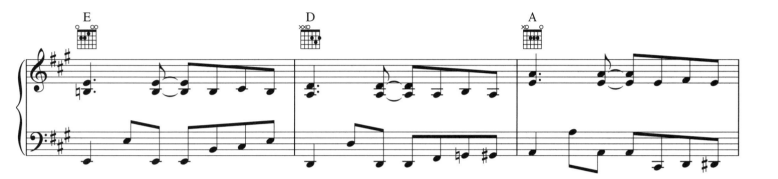

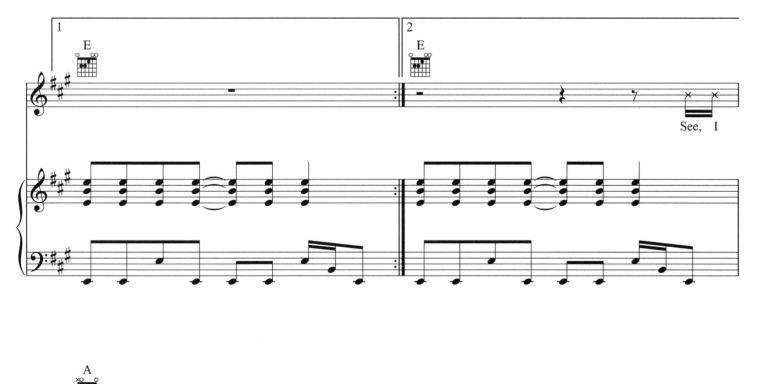

See, I

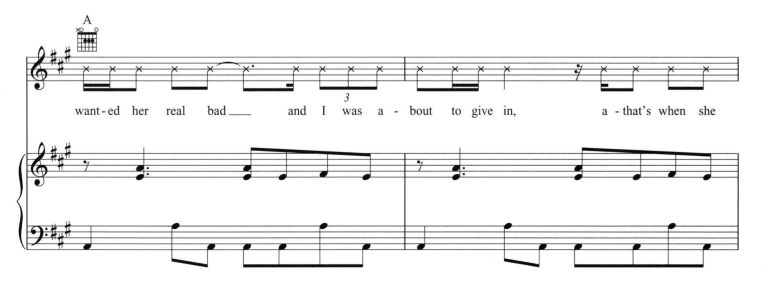

want-ed her real bad ____ and I was a - bout to give in, a - that's when she

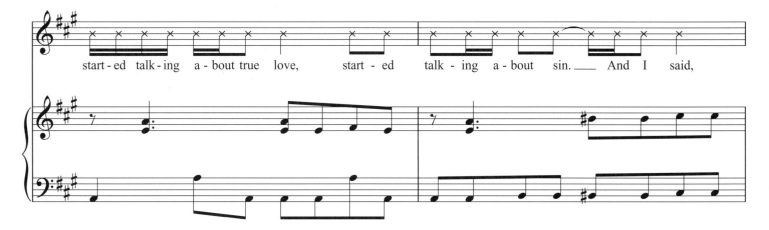

start - ed talk - ing a - bout true love, start - ed talk - ing a - bout sin. ___ And I said,

D

"Hon - ey, I'll live with you for the rest ___ of my life." ___ She said, "No

A

hug - ging, no kiss - ing un - til you make ___ me your wife." ___ My

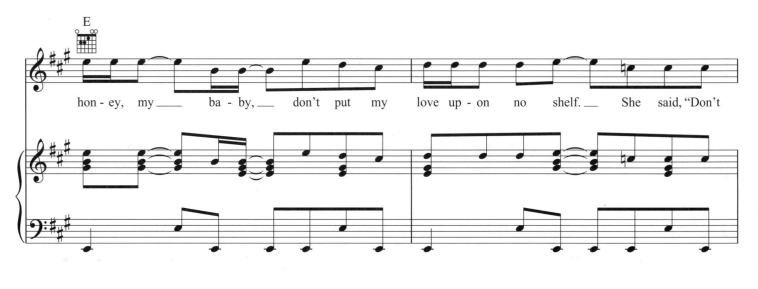

E

hon - ey, my ___ ba - by, ___ don't put my love up - on no shelf. ___ She said, "Don't

hand me no ___ lines, ___ and keep your hands to your - self." ___

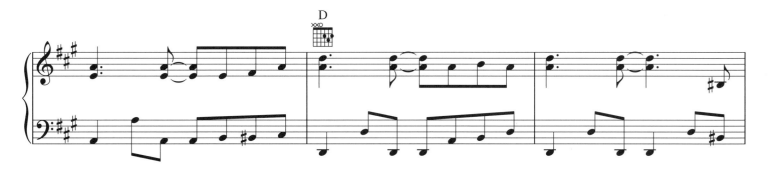

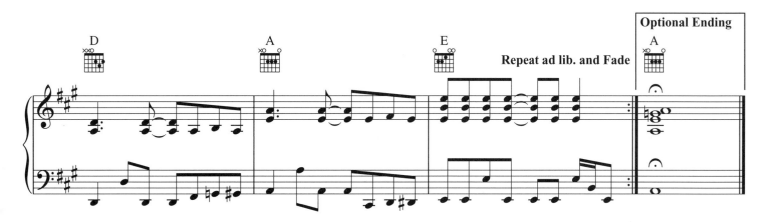

THE LAST THING ON MY MIND

Words and Music by
TOM PAXTON

1. It's a

1. les - son too late for the learn - ing, _____ made of
2.–4. *(See additional lyrics)*

sand, _____ made of sand. _____ In the

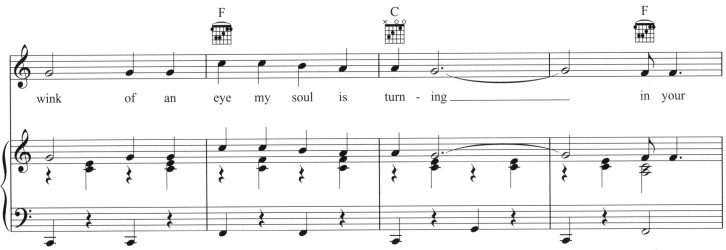

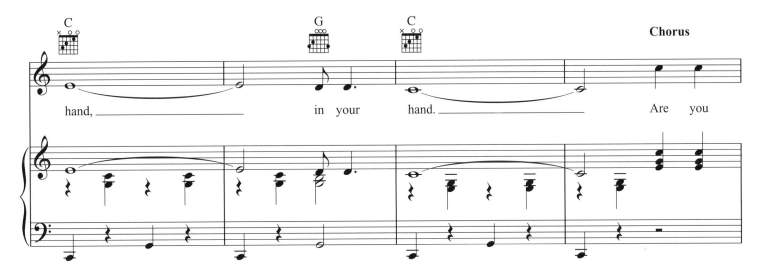

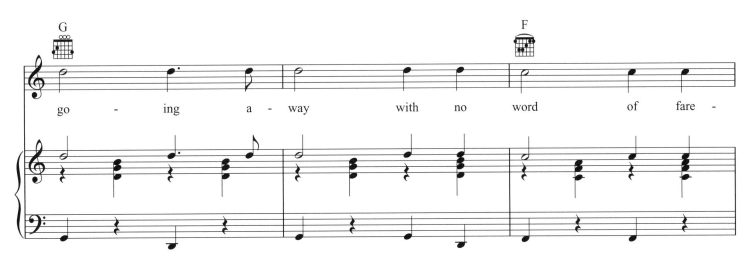

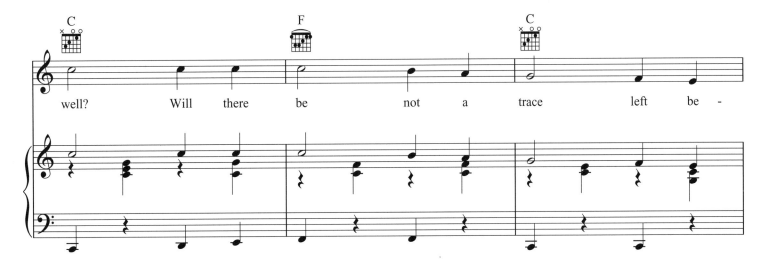

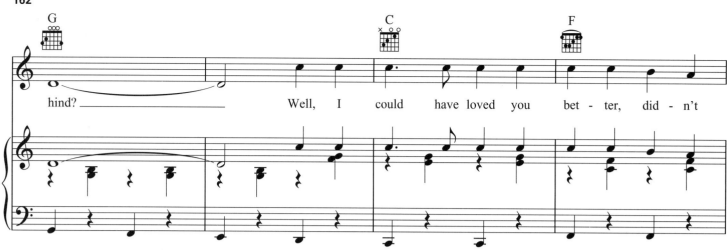

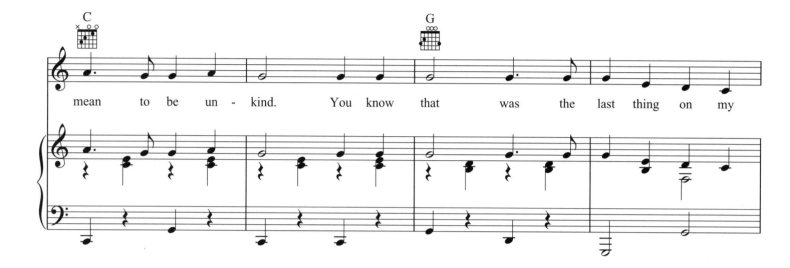

Additional Lyrics

2. As we walk, all my thoughts are a-tumblin'
'Round and 'round, 'round and 'round.
Underneath our feet the subway's rumblin'
Underground, underground.
Chorus

3. You've got reasons a-plenty for goin',
This I know, this I know.
For the weeds have been steadily growing.
Please don't go, please don't go.
Chorus

4. As I lie in my bed in the morning
Without you, without you,
Each song in my breast dies a-borning,
Without you, without you.
Chorus

LAST TRAIN TO CLARKSVILLE

Words and Music by BOBBY HART
and TOMMY BOYCE

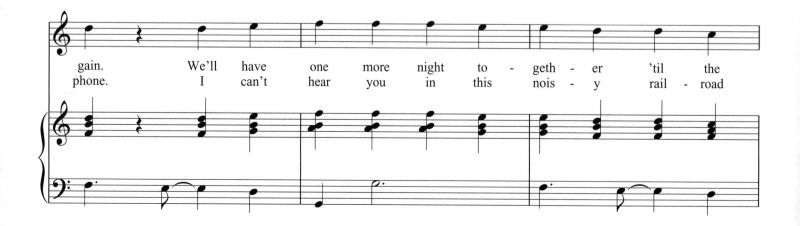

morn - ing brings my train. And I must go.
sta - tion all a - lone I'm feel - in' low.

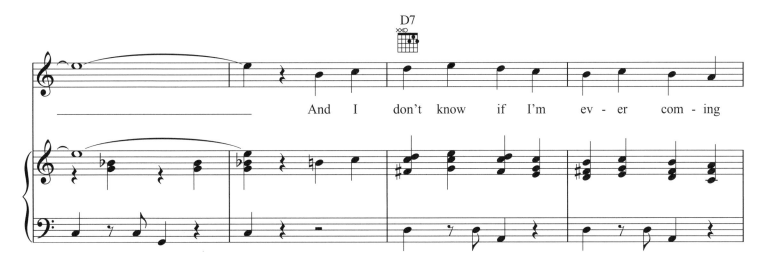

Oh, no, no, no! Oh, no, no, no!

And I don't know if I'm ev - er com - ing

2nd time D.S. and Fade

home. Take the

LAY DOWN SALLY

Words and Music by ERIC CLAPTON,
MARCY LEVY and GEORGE TERRY

Bright beat

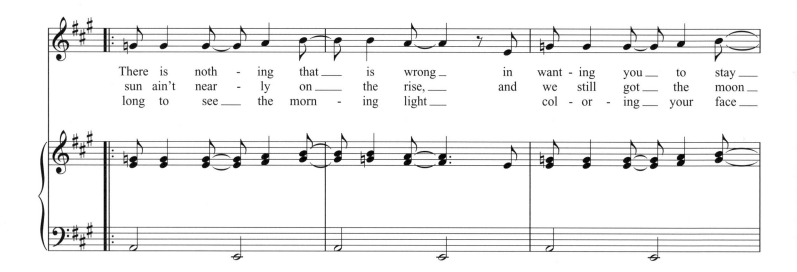

There is noth-ing that __ is wrong __ in want-ing you to stay __
sun ain't near-ly on __ the rise, __ and we still got __ the moon __
long to see __ the morn-ing light __ col-or-ing __ your face __

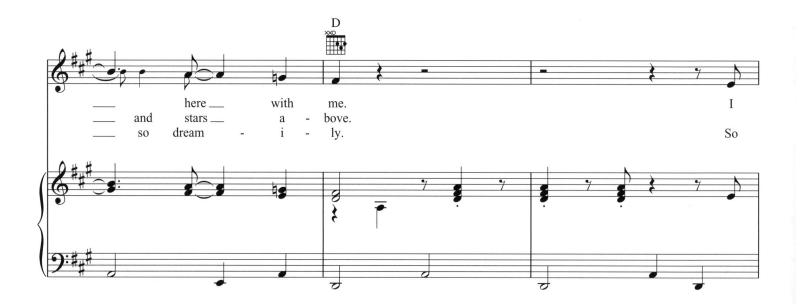

__ here __ with me.   I
__ and stars __ a-bove.   So
__ so dream-i-ly.

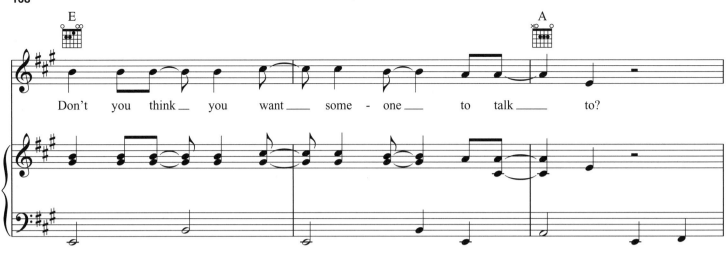

Don't you think__ you want__ some - one__ to talk__ to?

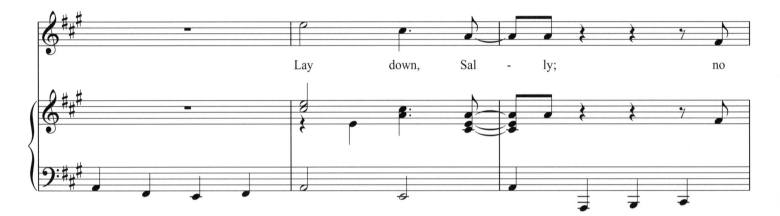

Lay down, Sal - ly; no

need to leave__ so soon.__ I've been try - ing all__

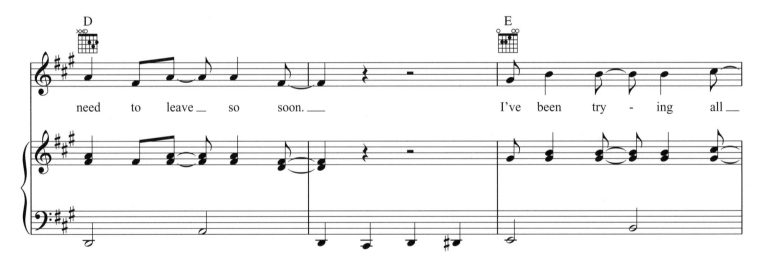

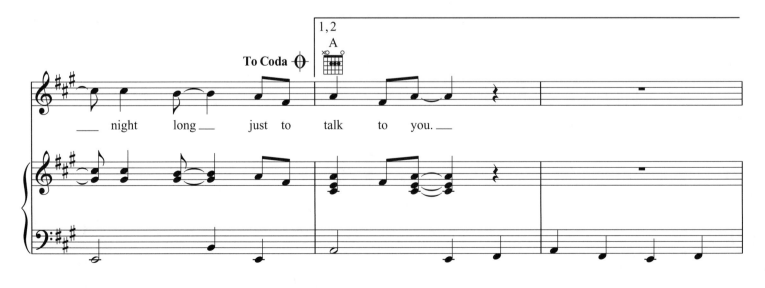

__ night long__ just to talk to you. __

The talk to you. __
I

talk to you. __

LEAVING ON A JET PLANE

Words and Music by
JOHN DENVER

dawn is break - in', it's ear - ly morn. _ The tax - i's wait - in', he's
place I go _ I'll think of you. _ Ev - 'ry song I sing _ I'll
Dream a - bout _ the days to come, _ when I won't have _ to

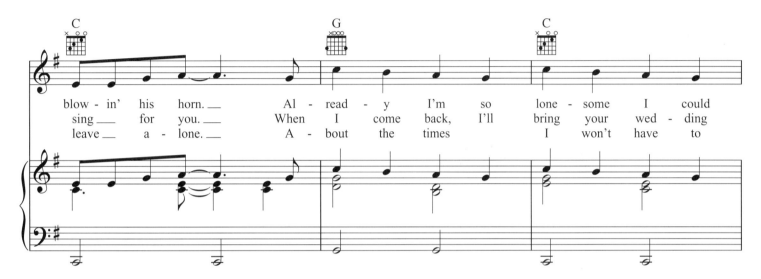

blow - in' his horn. _ Al - read - y I'm so lone - some I could
sing _ for you. _ When I come back, I'll bring your wed - ding
leave _ a - lone. _ A - bout the times I won't have to

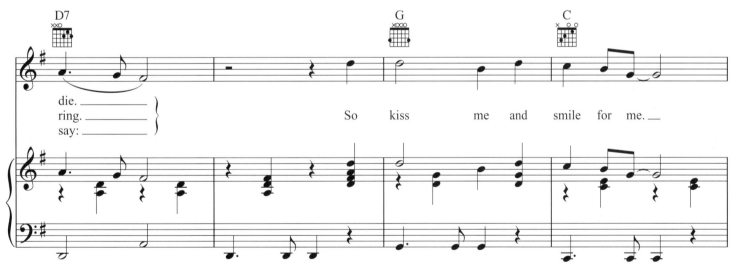

die. _____
ring. _____ } So kiss me and smile for me. _
say: _____

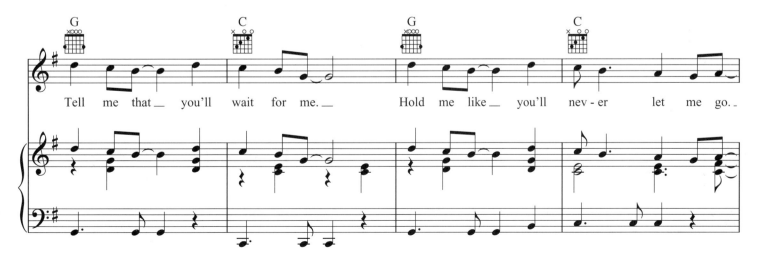

Tell me that _ you'll wait for me. _ Hold me like _ you'll nev - er let me go. _

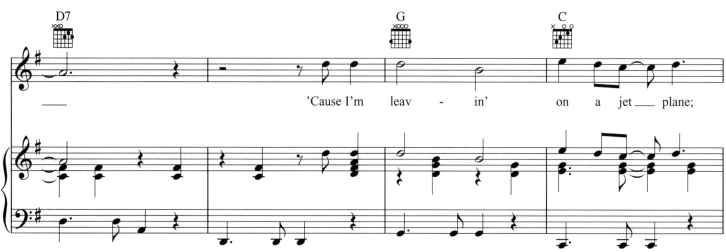

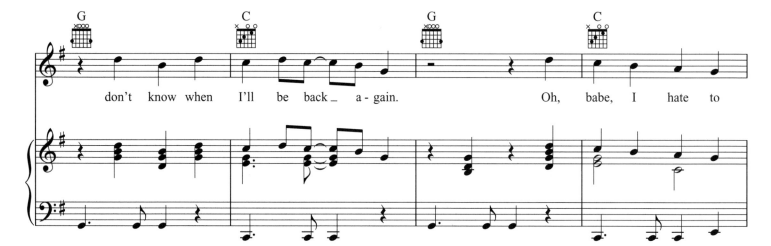

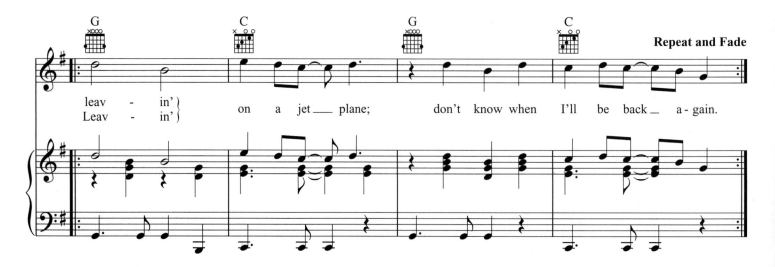

MUSTANG SALLY

Words and Music by
BONNY RICE

Moderate Blues Rock

Mus - tang   Sal - ly,

think you bet - ter   slow your   mus - tang   down.

Mus - tang

Sal - ly, think you better

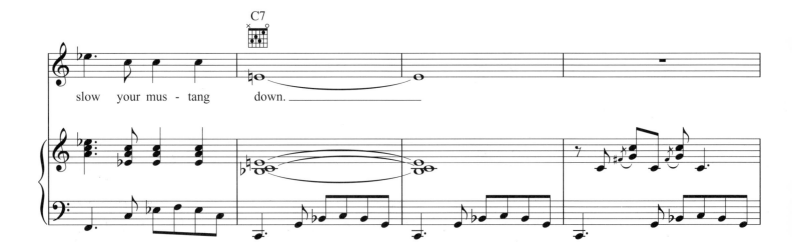

slow your mus - tang down. _____

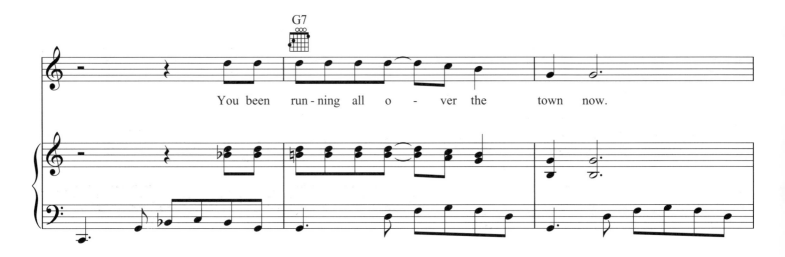

You been run - ning all o - ver the town now.

Oh! I guess I'll have to put your flat feet on the ground. _____

To Coda ⊕

All you want to do is ride a-round, Sal - ly. Ride, Sal - ly, ride. ___

All you want to do is ride a-round, Sal - ly. Ride, Sal - ly, ride. _

___ All you want to do is ride a-round, Sal - ly.

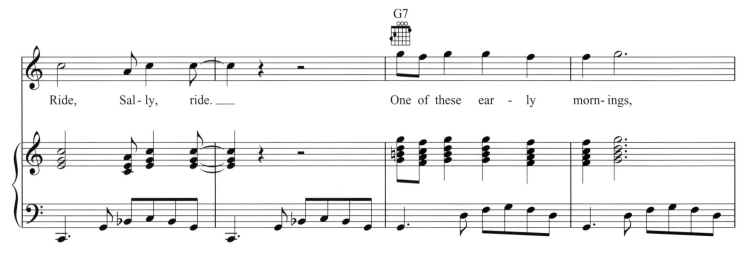

Ride, Sal-ly, ride.____ One of these ear-ly morn-ings,

oh, you gon-na be wip-ing your weep-ing____ eyes.____

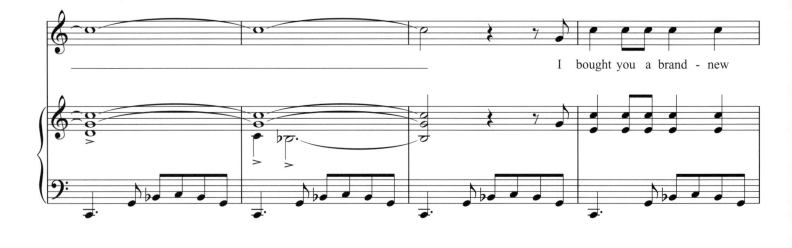

I bought you a brand-new

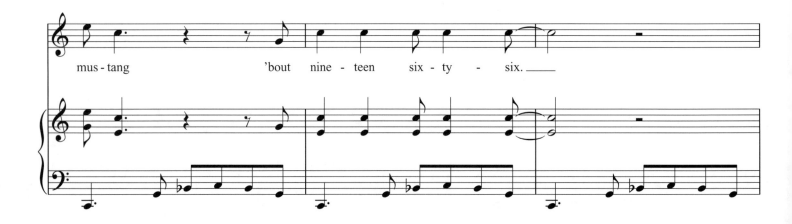

mus-tang 'bout nine-teen six-ty - six.____

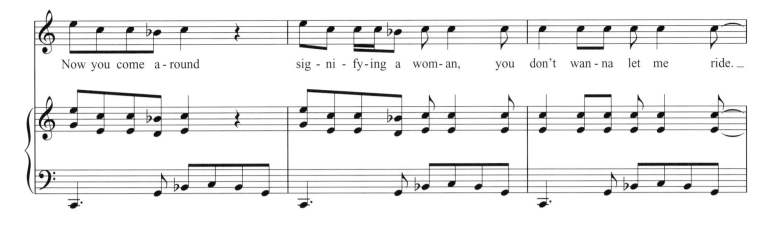

Now you come a - round sig - ni - fy-ing a wom-an, you don't wan-na let me ride.

D.S. al Coda

Mus - tang

CODA

C7

All you want to do is ride a - round, Sal - ly.

Optional Ending

Repeat and Fade

C7

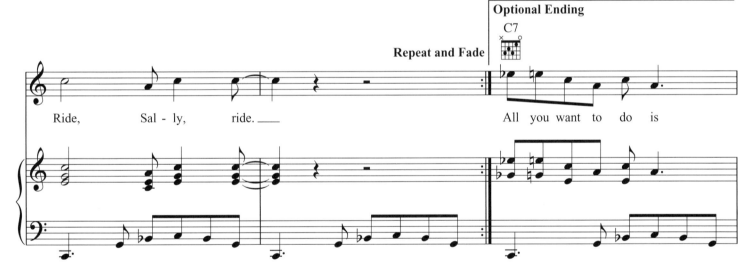

Ride, Sal - ly, ride. All you want to do is

ride a - round, Sal - ly. Ride, Sal - ly, ride.

LOUIE, LOUIE

Words and Music by
RICHARD BERRY

Medium Rock beat

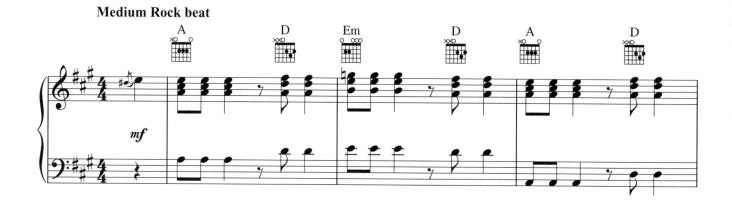

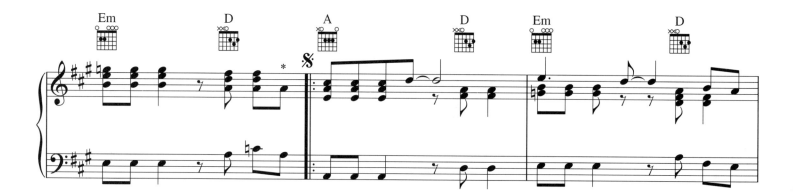

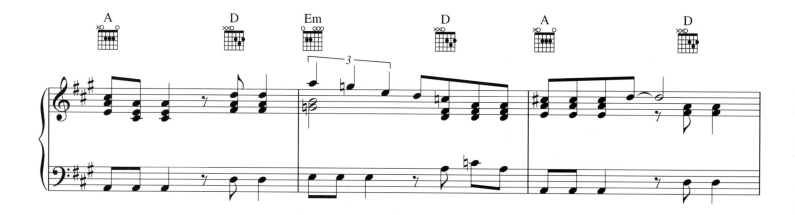

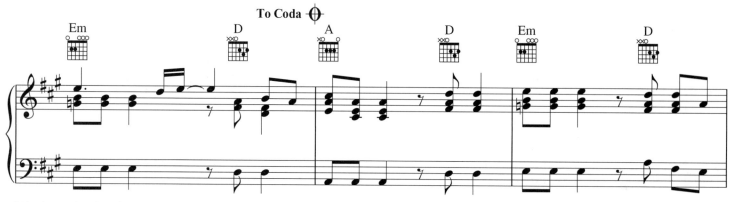

* Lyrics omitted at the request of the publisher.

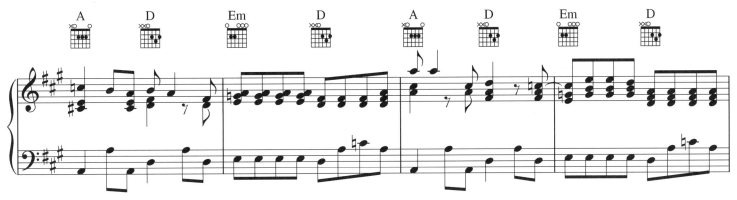

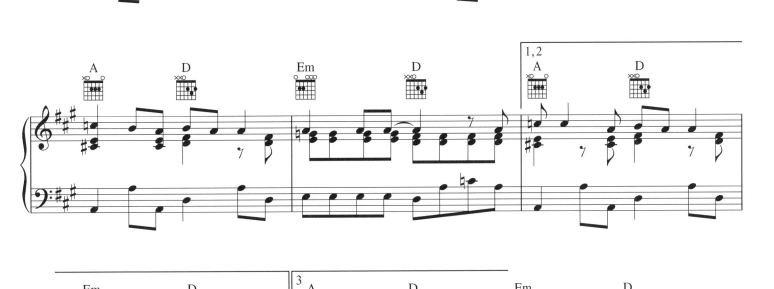

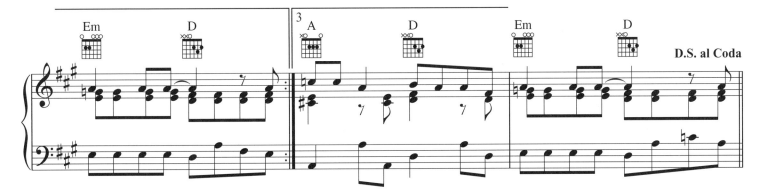

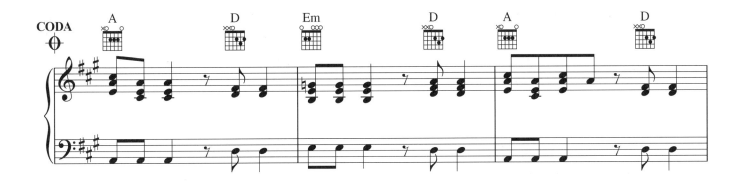

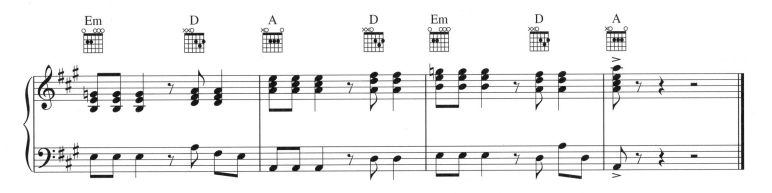

MAMA TRIED

Words and Music by
MERLE HAGGARD

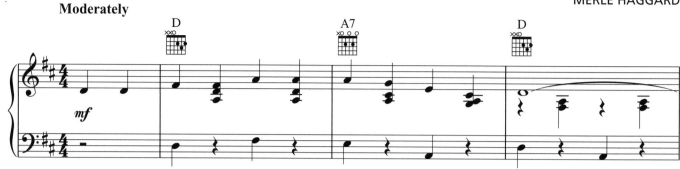

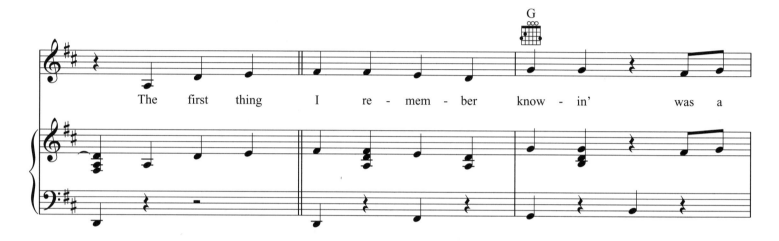

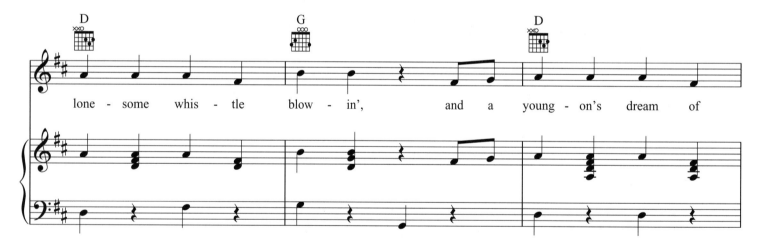

The first thing I re-mem-ber know-in' was a lone-some whis-tle blow-in', and a young-on's dream of

grow-in' up to ride _____ on a freight train leav-in'

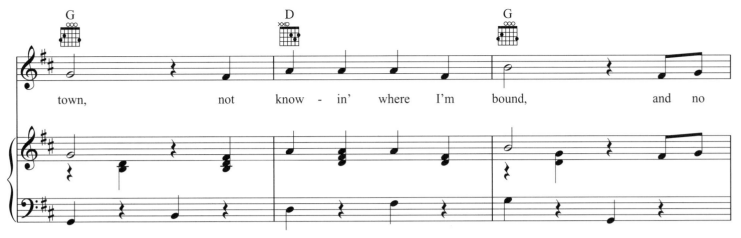

town,   not know - in' where I'm bound,   and no

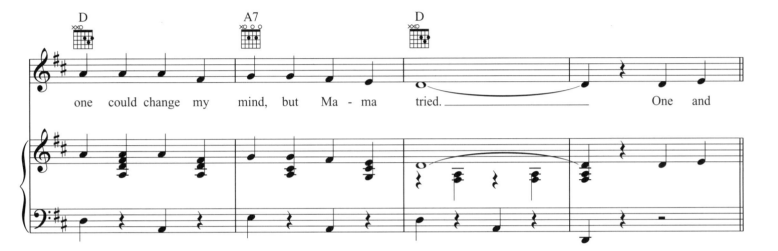

one could change my mind, but Ma - ma tried. _____ One and

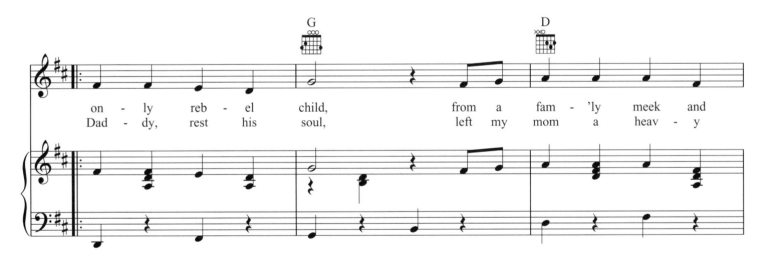

on - ly reb - el child,   from a fam - 'ly meek and
Dad - dy, rest his soul,   left my mom a heav - y

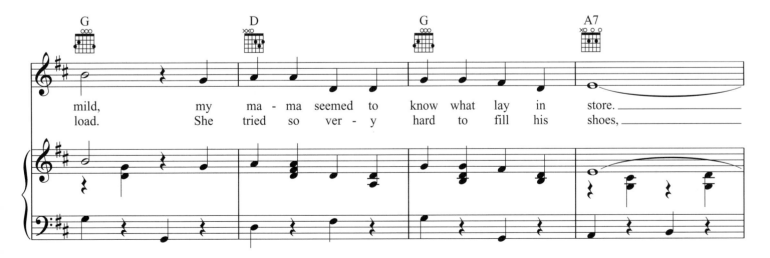

mild,   my ma - ma seemed to know what lay in store. _____
load.   She tried so ver - y hard to fill his shoes, _____

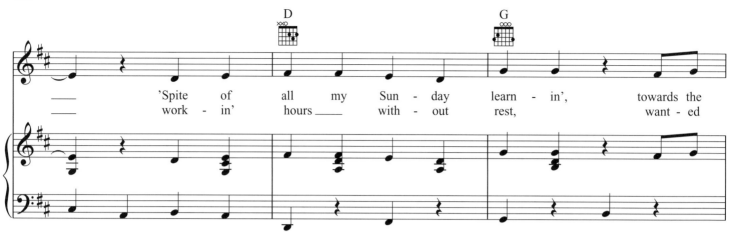

'Spite of all my Sun-day learn-in', towards the
work-in' all hours ___ with-out rest, want-ed

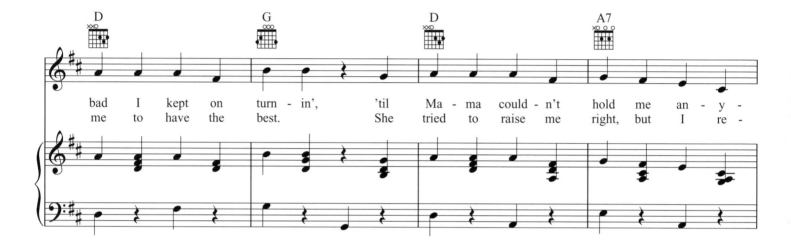

bad I kept on turn-in', 'til Ma-ma could-n't hold me an-y-
me to have the best. She tried to raise me right, but I re-

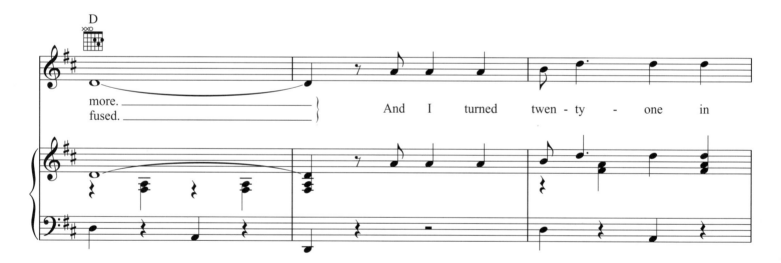

more. ___
fused. ___

And I turned twen-ty-one in

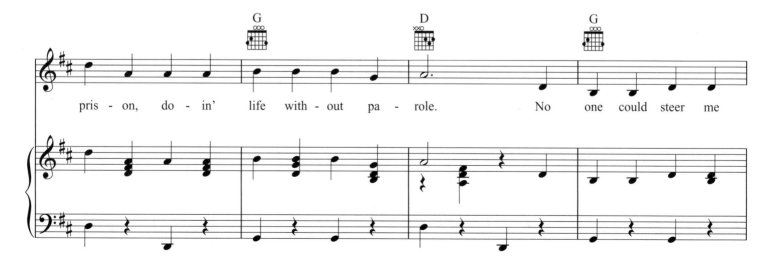

pris-on, do-in' life with-out pa-role. No one could steer me

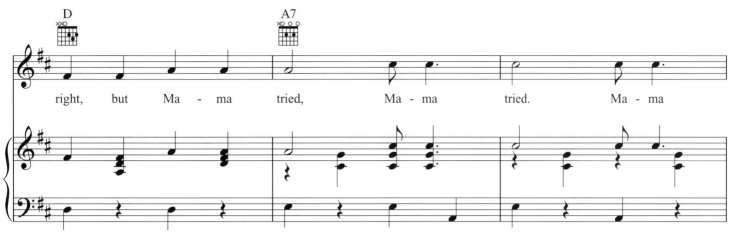

right, but Ma - ma tried, Ma - ma tried. Ma - ma

tried to raise me bet - ter, but her plead - ing I de -

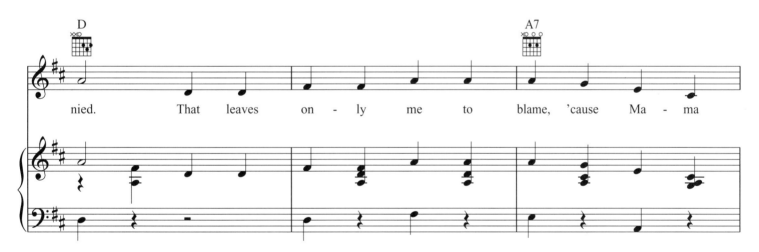

nied. That leaves on - ly me to blame, 'cause Ma - ma

tried. _____ Dear ol' tried. _____

ME AND BOBBY McGEE

Words and Music by KRIS KRISTOFFERSON
and FRED FOSTER

Bob - by thumbed a die - sel down just be - fore it rained;
stand - in' right be - side me, Lord, through ev - 'ry - thing I done,

took us all the way to New Or - leans.
ev - 'ry night she kept me from the cold. Then

I took my har - poon out of my dirt - y red ban - dan - na and was
some - where near Sa - li - nas, Lord, I let her slip a - way,

blow - in' sad while Bob - by sang the blues. With them
look - in' for the home I hope she'll find. And I'd trade

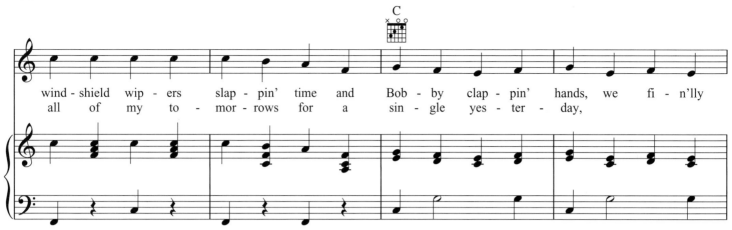

C

wind - shield wip - ers slap - pin' time and Bob - by clap - pin' hands, we fi - n'lly
all of my to - mor - rows for a sin - gle yes - ter - day,

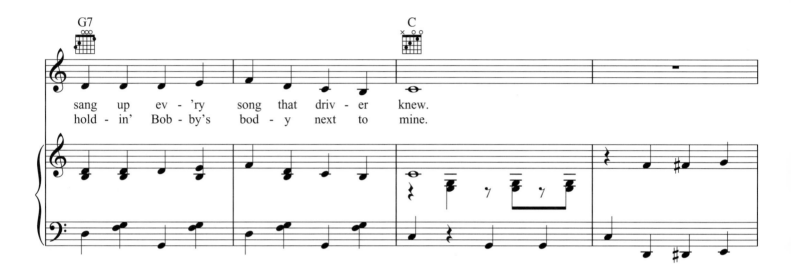

G7   C

sang up ev - 'ry song that driv - er knew.
hold - in' Bob - by's bod - y next to mine.

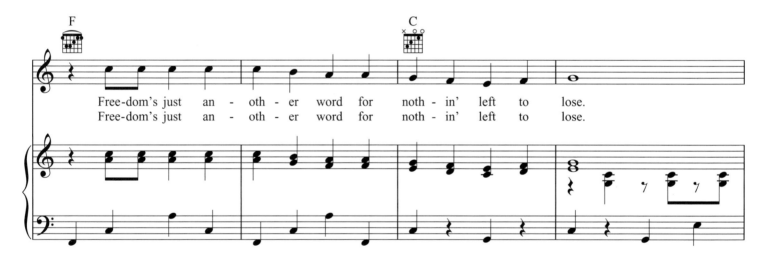

F   C

Free - dom's just an - oth - er word for noth - in' left to lose.
Free - dom's just an - oth - er word for noth - in' left to lose.

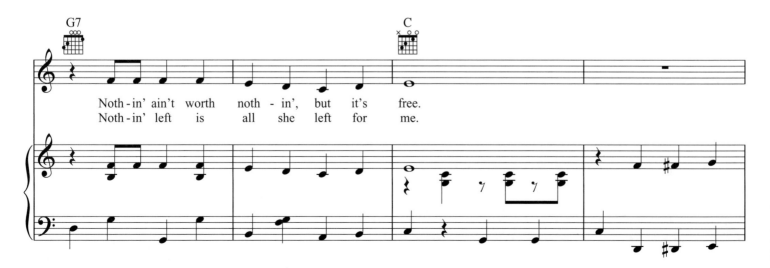

G7   C

Noth - in' ain't worth noth - in', but it's free.
Noth - in' left is all she left for me.

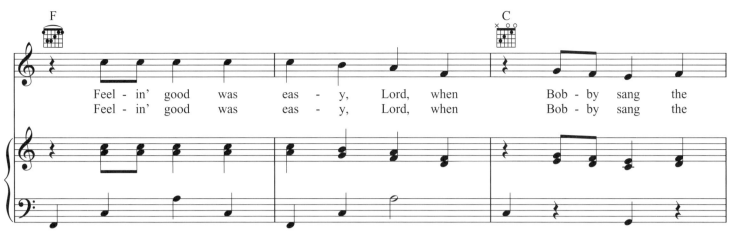

Feel - in' good was eas - y, Lord, when Bob - by sang the
Feel - in' good was eas - y, Lord, when Bob - by sang the

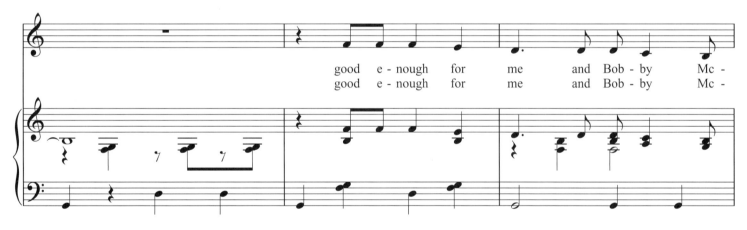

blues; and feel - in' good was good e - nough for me,
blues; And, bud - dy, that was good e - nough for me,

good e - nough for me and Bob - by Mc -
good e - nough for me and Bob - by Mc -

Gee. From the Gee.

MOVE IT ON OVER

Words and Music by
HANK WILLIAMS

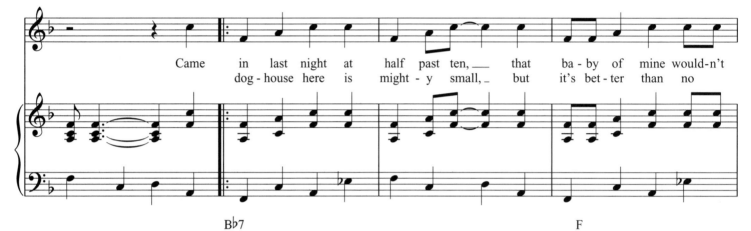

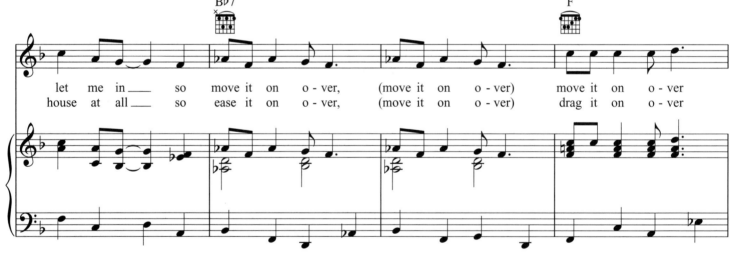

in. _____ She changed the lock on our front door,_ now
in. _____ She told me not to play a - round_ but

my door key don't fit no more._ So get it on o - ver, (move it on o - ver)
I done let the deal go down._ So pack it on o - ver, (move it on o - ver)

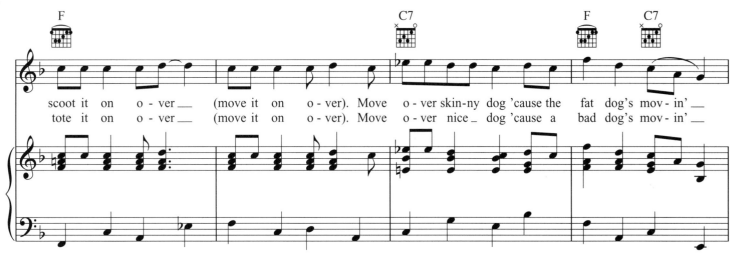

scoot it on o - ver __ (move it on o - ver). Move o - ver skin-ny dog 'cause the fat dog's mov-in' __
tote it on o - ver __ (move it on o - ver). Move o - ver nice _ dog 'cause a bad dog's mov-in' __

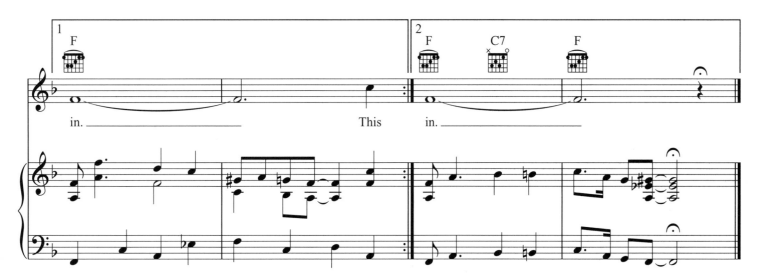

in. _____ This in. _____

OLD TIME ROCK & ROLL

Words and Music by GEORGE JACKSON
and THOMAS E. JONES III

Moderate Rock 'n' Roll beat

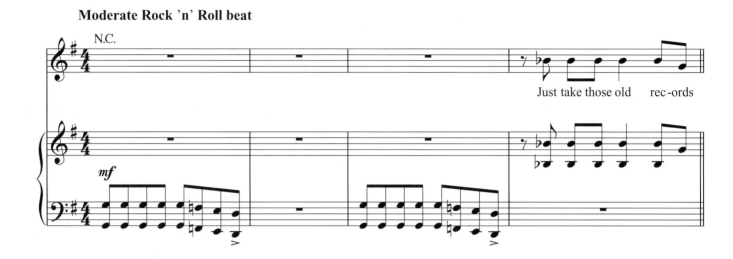

Just take those old rec-ords

off the shelf. ___ I'll sit and lis-ten to 'em by my-self. ___
tan - go. _____ I'd rath-er hear some blues or funk-y old soul. ___

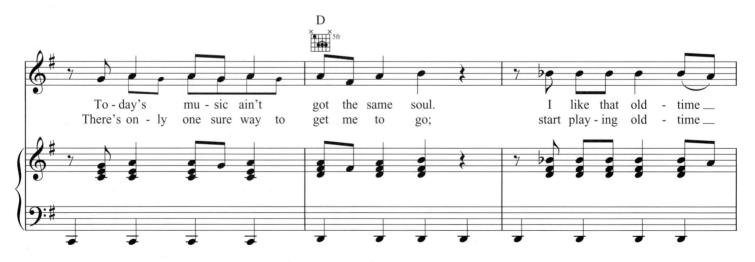

To-day's mu-sic ain't got the same soul. I like that old - time ___
There's on - ly one sure way to get me to go; start play-ing old - time ___

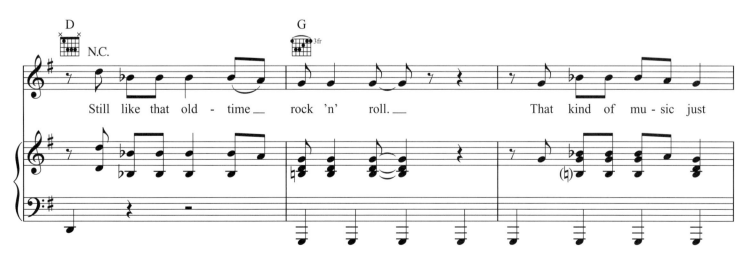

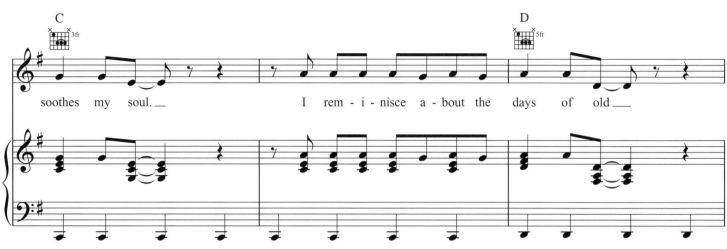

soothes my soul.___ I rem - i - nisce a - bout the days of old ___

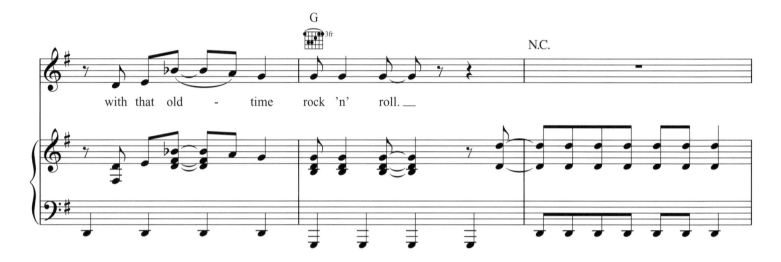

with that old - time rock 'n' roll.___

N.C.

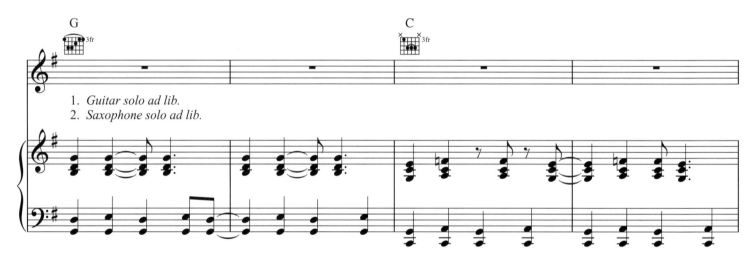

1. *Guitar solo ad lib.*
2. *Saxophone solo ad lib.*

RING OF FIRE

Words and Music by MERLE KILGORE
and JUNE CARTER

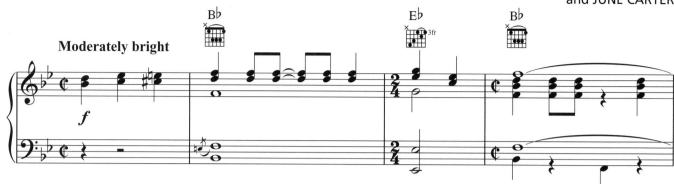

Moderately bright

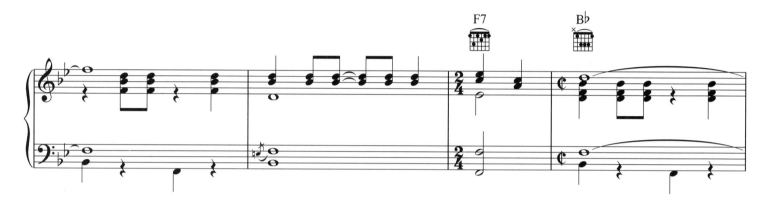

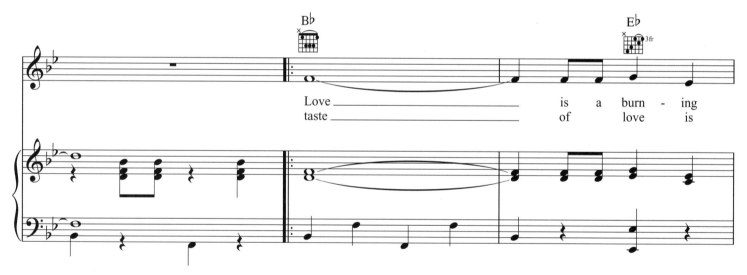

Love _____ is a burn - ing
taste _____ of love is

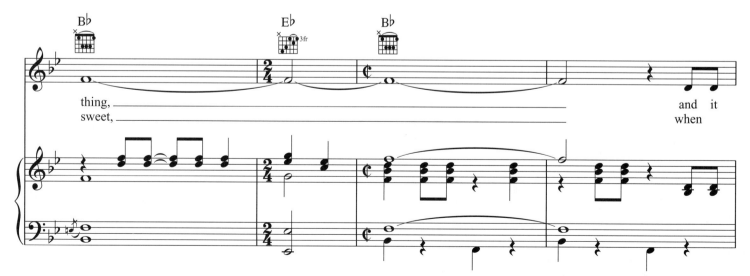

thing, _____ and it
sweet, _____ when

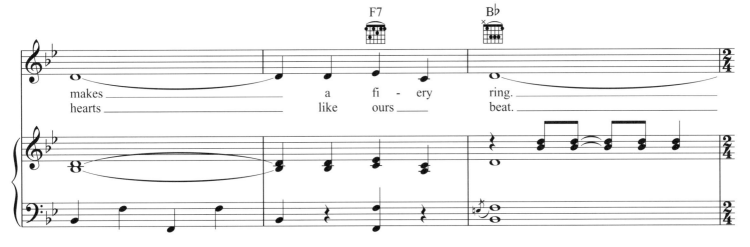

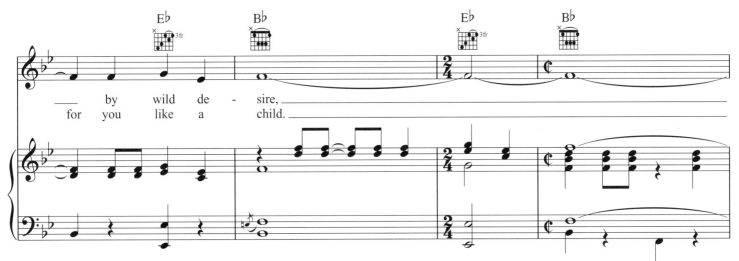

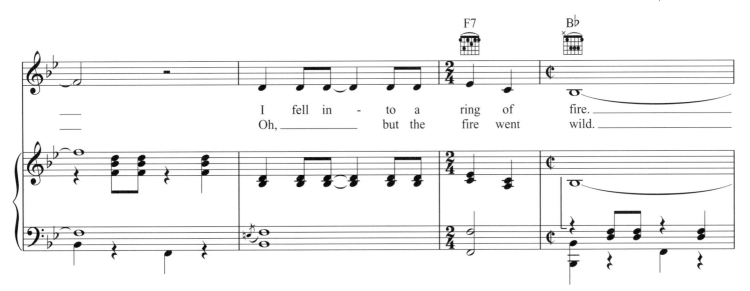

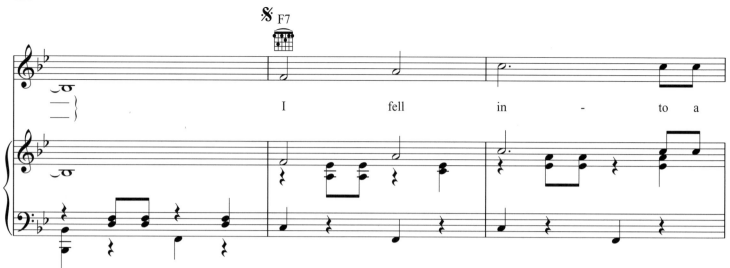

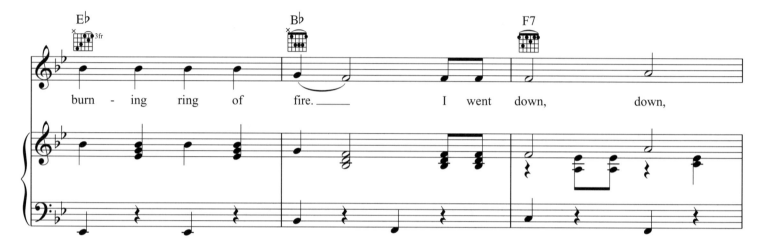

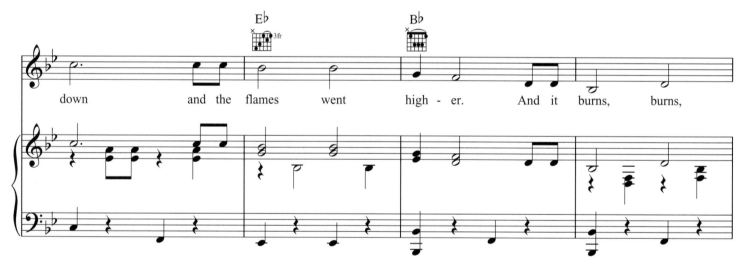

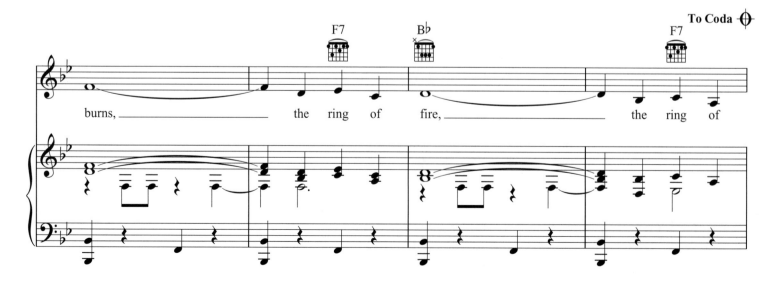

ROYALS

Words and Music by ELLA YELICH-O'CONNOR
and JOEL LITTLE

Moderately

I've nev-er seen a dia-mond in the flesh. _____
I, we've cracked the code. _____

I cut my teeth on wed-ding rings _____ in the
We count our dol-lars on the train _____ to the

mov-ies. _____ And I'm not proud of my ad-dress. _____
par-ty. _____ And ev-'ry-one who knows us knows _____

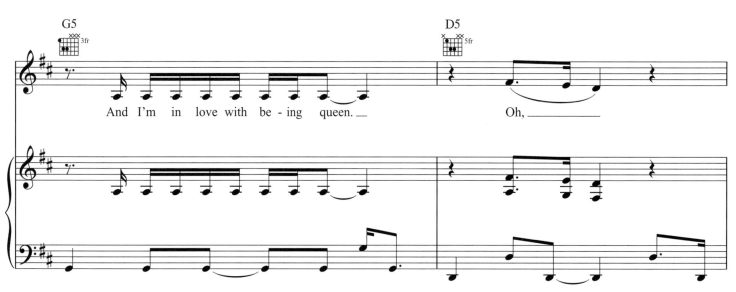

And I'm in love with be - ing queen. ___ Oh, ___

oh, ___ oh, ___ life is great with - out a care. ___ We aren't

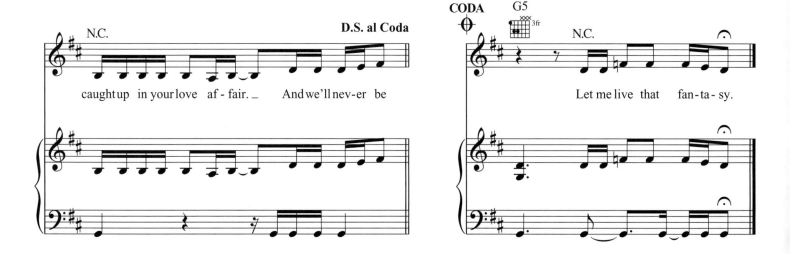

caught up in your love af - fair. ___ And we'll nev-er be

Let me live that fan - ta - sy.

READY TEDDY

Words and Music by JOHN MARASCALCO
and ROBERT BLACKWELL

Bright tempo

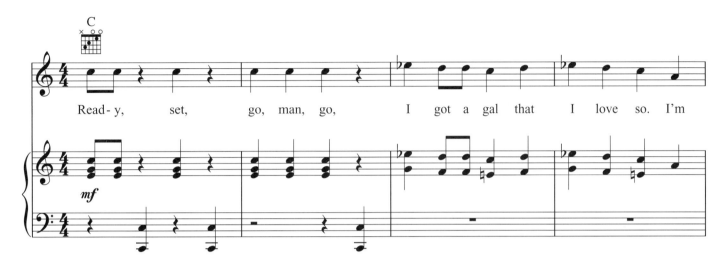

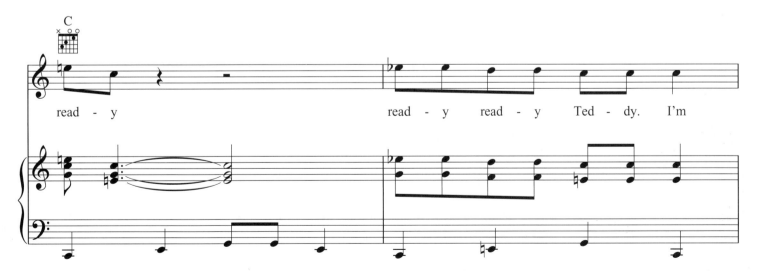

ready ready ready Ted - dy. I'm

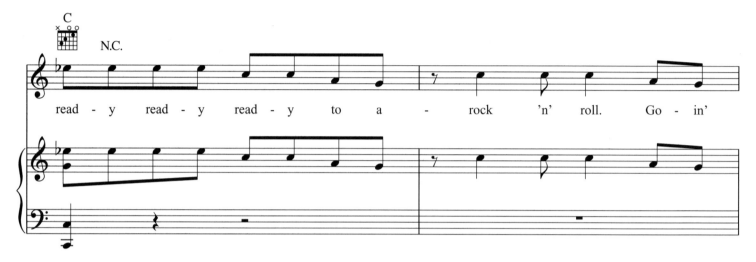

read - y read - y read - y to a - rock 'n' roll. Go - in'

down to the cor - ner, pick up _____ my sweet - ie pie. She's my

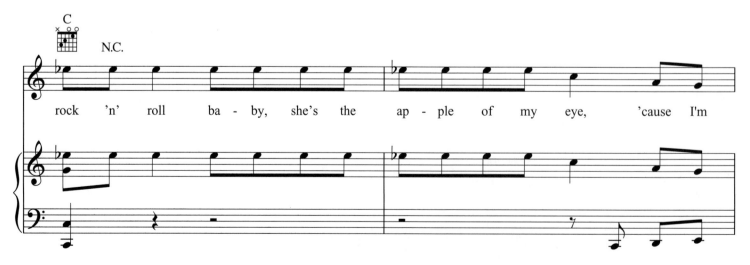

rock 'n' roll ba - by, she's the ap - ple of my eye, 'cause I'm

read - y   read - y read - y Ted - dy. I'm

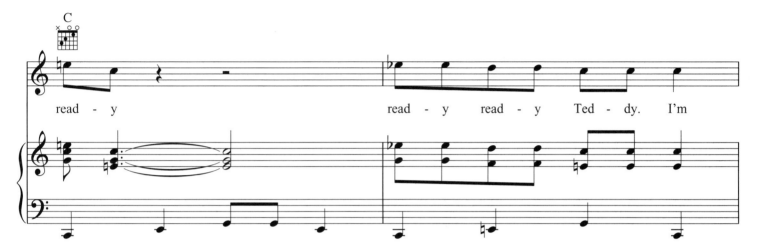

read - y   read - y read - y Ted - dy. I'm

read - y   read - y read - y Ted - dy. I'm

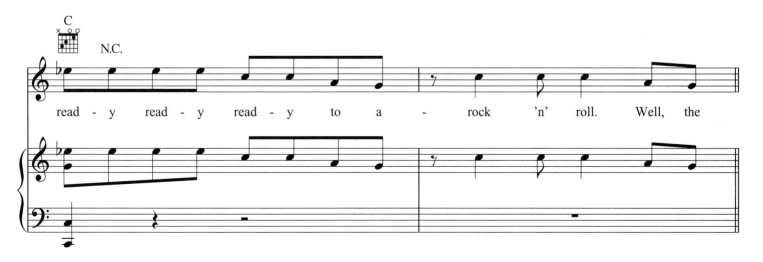

read - y read - y read - y to a - rock 'n' roll. Well, the

flat - top cats and the dun - ga - ree dolls are ____
kick off my shoes, roll ____ up my fad - ed jeans. Grab my

head - ed for the gym to the Sock Hop Ball. ____ The
rock 'n' roll ba - by, pour ____ on the steam. ____ I

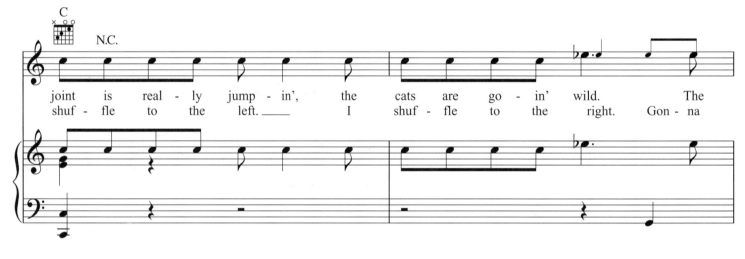

joint is real - ly jump - in', the cats are go - in' wild. The
shuf - fle to the left. ____ I shuf - fle to the right. Gon - na

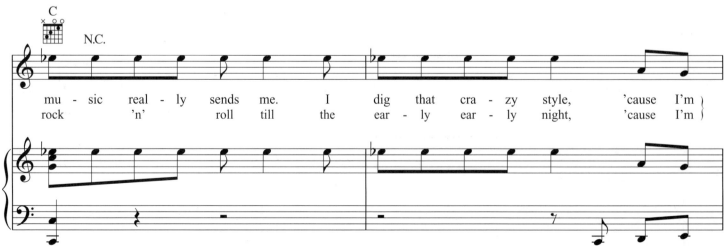

mu - sic real - ly sends me. I dig that cra - zy style, 'cause I'm }
rock 'n' roll till the ear - ly ear - ly night, 'cause I'm }

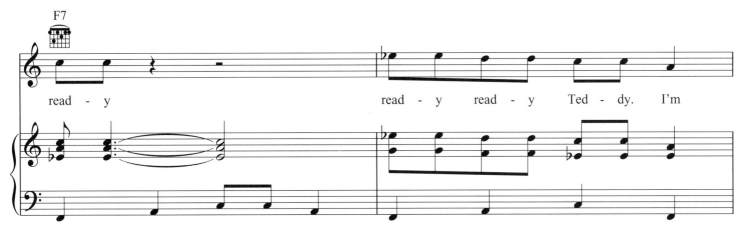

read - y read - y read - y Ted - dy. I'm

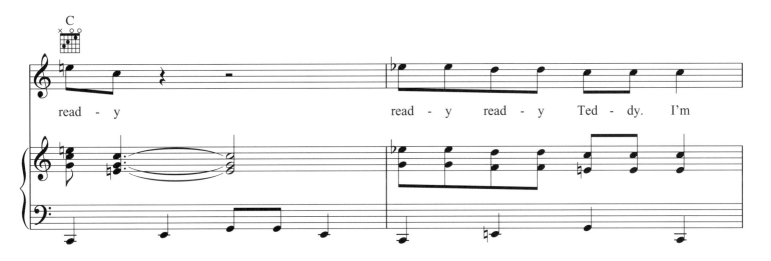

read - y read - y read - y Ted - dy. I'm

read - y read - y read - y Ted - dy. I'm

read - y read - y read - y to a - rock 'n' roll. Gon - na - rock 'n' roll.

SEVEN BRIDGES ROAD

Words and Music by
STEPHEN T. YOUNG

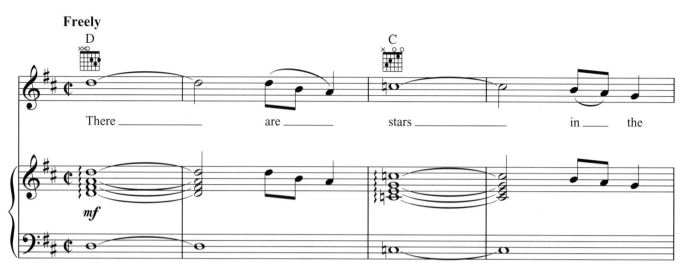

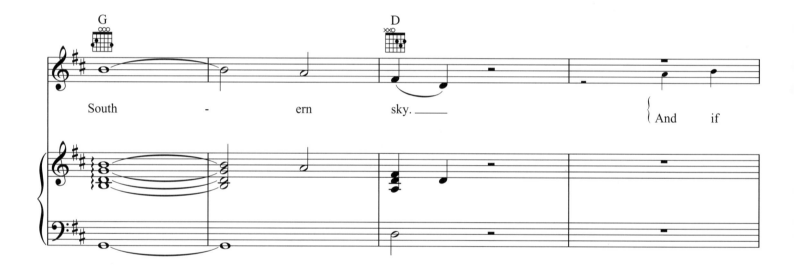

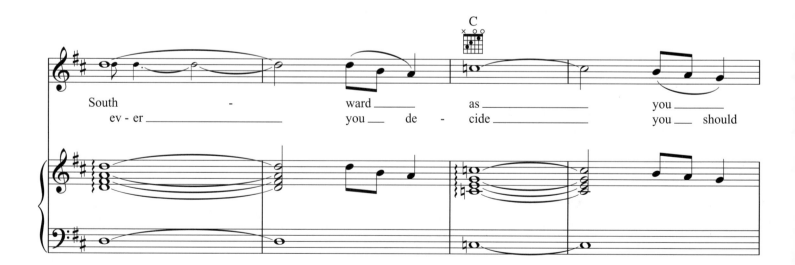

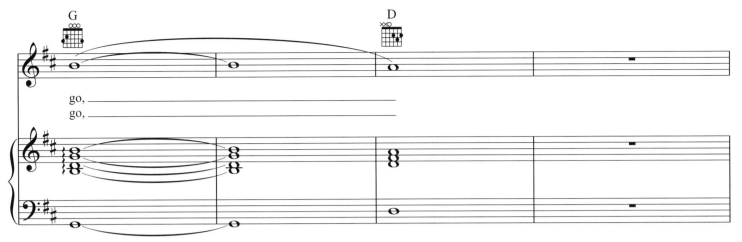

go, _____

go, _____

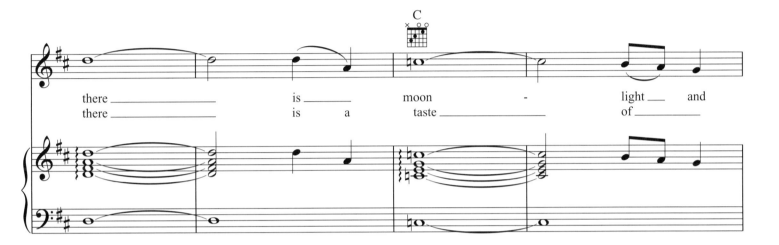

there _____ is _____ moon - light ___ and

there _____ is a taste _____ of _____

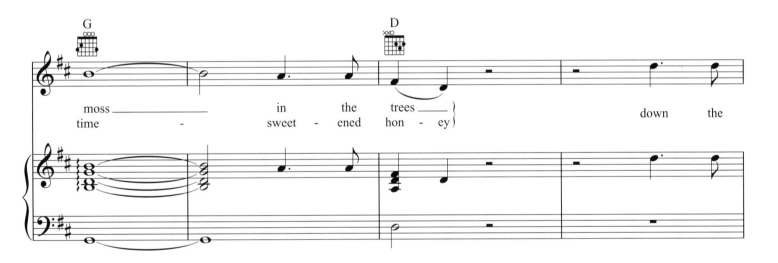

moss _____ in the trees ___ down the

time - sweet - ened hon - ey down the

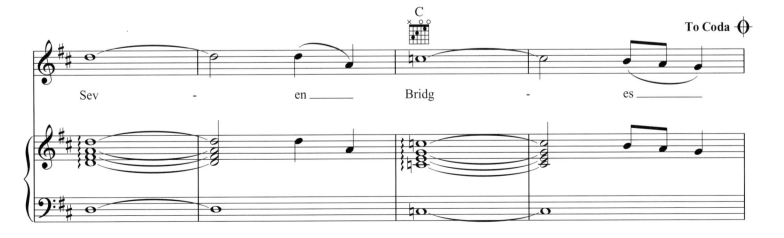

To Coda ⊕

Sev - en _____ Bridg - es _____

Bright Country

Road.

Now, I _____ have _____
I _____ have _____

loved _____ you _____
loved _____ you _____

_____ like a ba - by, like _____
_____ in a tame _____ way and I _____

some   lone   some   child.
have   loved   you   wild.

And   Some - times

there's   a part

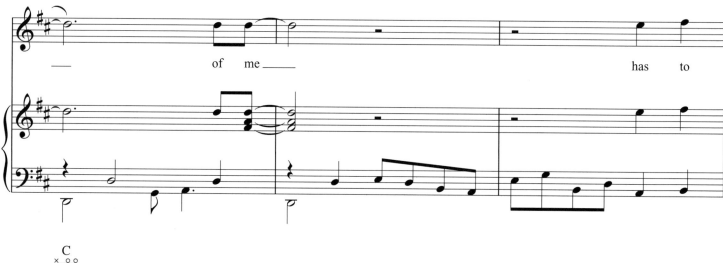

of me _____ has to

C

turn _____ from here _____ and

D

go,

C

run - ning _____ like a child _____ from

these _____ warm stars down the

Sev - en _____ Bridg - es _____

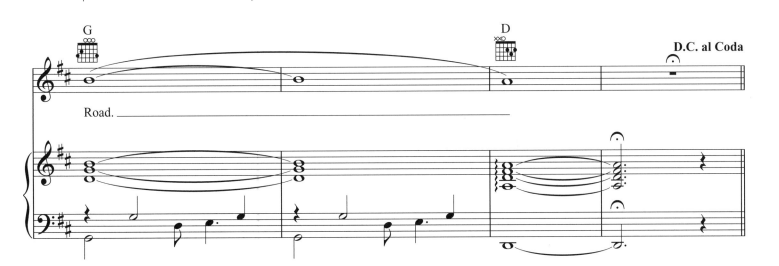

Road. _____

D.C. al Coda

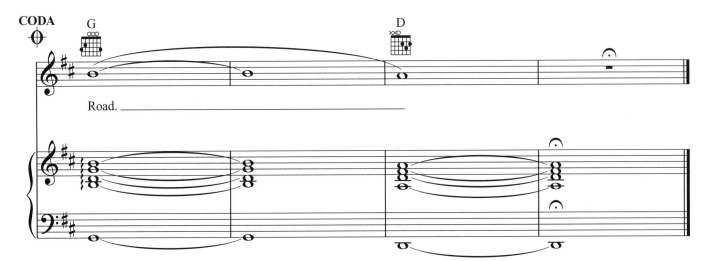

CODA

Road. _____

SHAKE IT OFF

Words and Music by TAYLOR SWIFT,
MAX MARTIN and SHELLBACK

at least, that's what peo - ple say, _____ mm, mm. That's what peo - ple
And that's what they don't know, _____ mm, mm. That's what they don't

say, _____ mm, mm. But I keep cruis - ing;
know, _____ mm, mm. But I keep cruis - ing;

Am7

can't stop, won't stop mov - ing.} It's like I got this
can't stop, won't stop groov - ing.} It's like I got this

C

N.C.

mu - sic in my mind say - ing, "It's gon - na be al - right." _

off. I, I, I shake it off, I shake it off. ___
(Ooh, ___ ooh!)

N.C.

1. *Spoken: (See additional lyrics)*
2. Rap: *(See additional lyrics)*

1

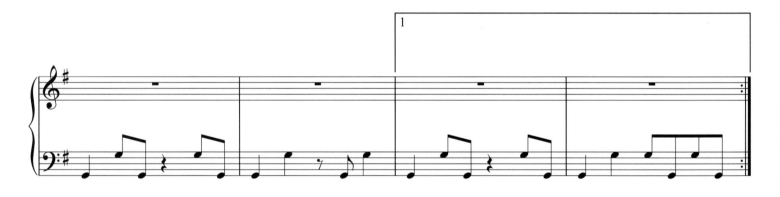

2

D.S. al Coda

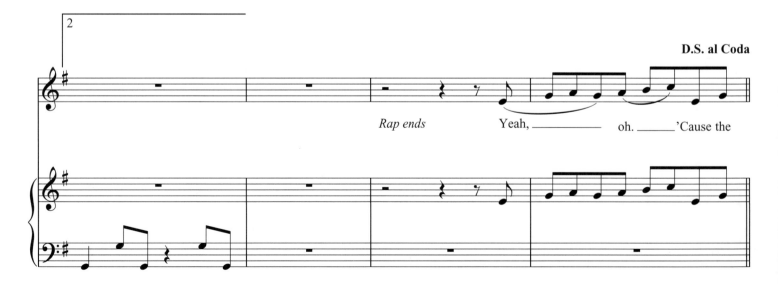

Rap ends   Yeah, _____ oh. _____ 'Cause the

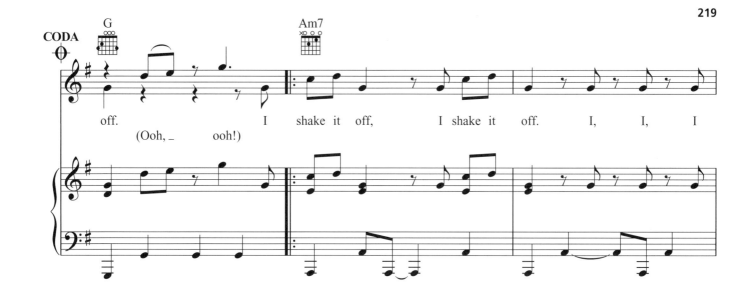

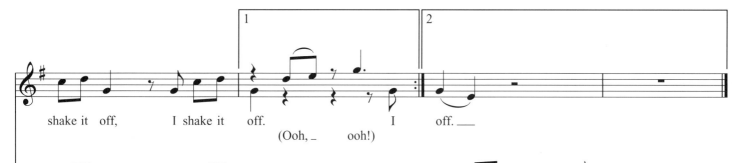

Additional Lyrics

Spoken: *Hey, hey, hey! Just think: While you've been getting*
Down and out about the liars and the dirty, dirty
Cheats of the world, you could've been getting down to
This. Sick. Beat!

Rap: My ex-man brought his new girlfriend.
She's like, "Oh, my god!" But I'm just gonna shake.
And to the fella over there with the hella good hair,
Won't you come on over, baby? We can shake, shake, shake.

STUCK ON YOU

Words and Music by AARON SCHROEDER
and J.L. McFARLAND

Moderately

You can shake an ap-ple off an ap-ple tree. _
Gon-na run my fin-gers through your long black hair. _

Shake-a shake-a, sug-ar, but you'll nev-er shake me. _ Uh-uh-uh. _
Squeeze _ you _ tight-er than a griz-ly bear. _ Uh-huh-huh. _

No, sir-ee, _ uh-uh. _ I'm gon-na
Yes, sir-ee, _ uh-huh. _ I'm gon-na

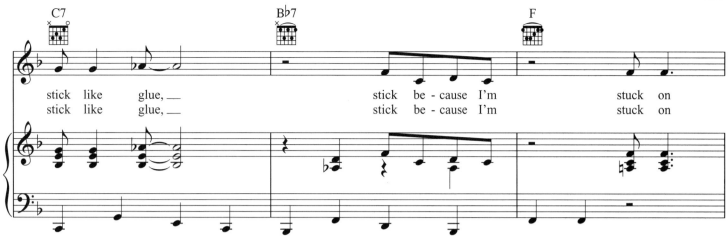

stick like   glue, ___   stick   be - cause   I'm   stuck   on
stick like   glue, ___   stick   be - cause   I'm   stuck   on

you.   you.   Hide in the kitch - en,   hide   in   the   hall,

ain't gon - na   do   you   no   good   at   all. ___   'Cause   once   I   catch   ya   and   the

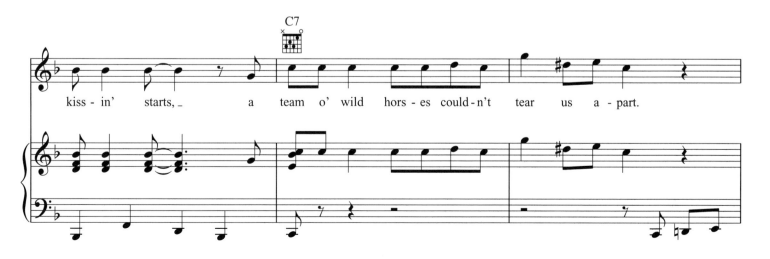

kiss - in'   starts, ___   a   team   o'   wild   hors - es   could - n't   tear   us   a - part.

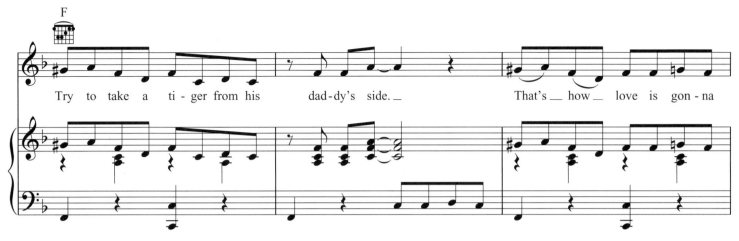

Try to take a ti-ger from his dad-dy's side. ___ That's ___ how ___ love is gon-na

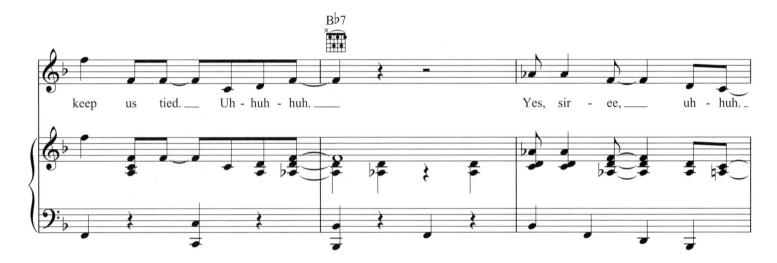

keep us tied. ___ Uh - huh - huh. ___ Yes, sir - ee, ___ uh - huh. ___

I'm gon-na stick like glue, ___

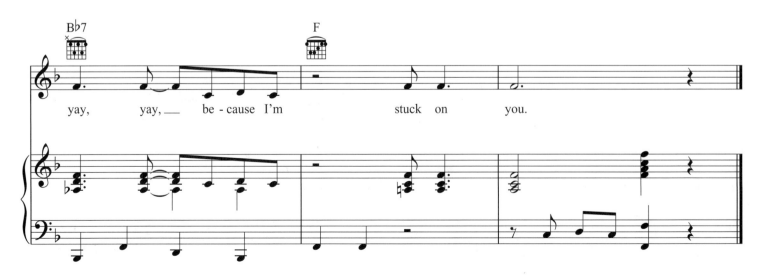

yay, yay, ___ be - cause I'm stuck on you.

STIR IT UP

Words and Music by
BOB MARLEY

Moderate Reggae

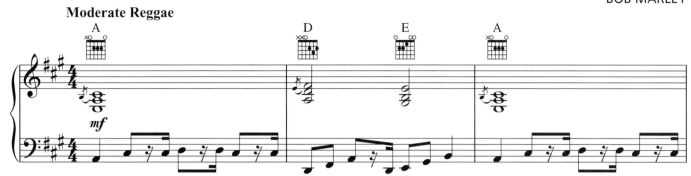

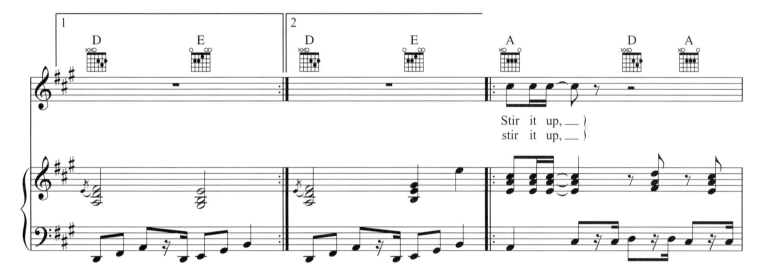

Stir it up, ___
stir it up, ___

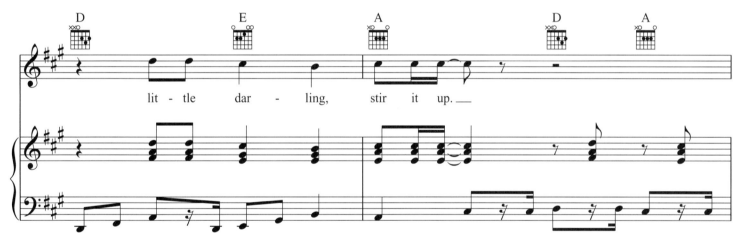

lit - tle dar - ling, stir it up. ___

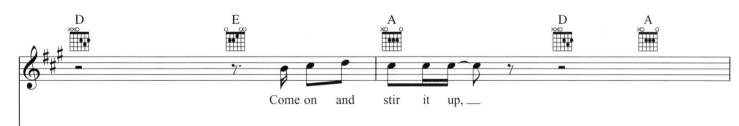

Come on and stir it up, ___

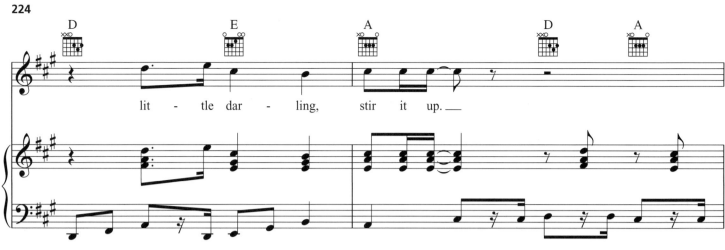

lit - tle dar - ling, stir it up. ___

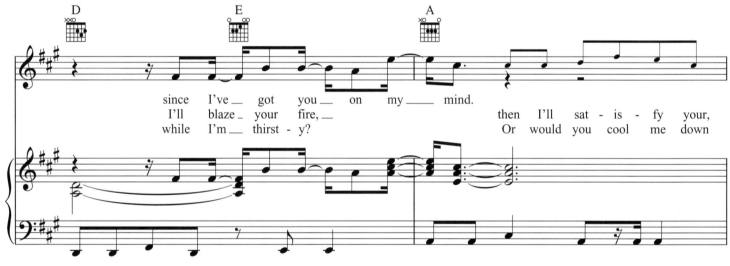

It's been a long, ___ long time ___
I'll push ___ the wood, ___
Oh, will you quench me ___

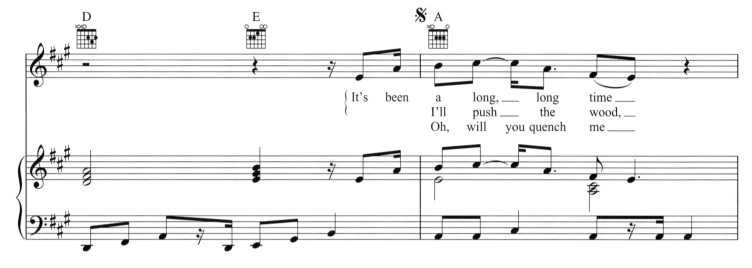

since I've ___ got you ___ on my ___ mind.
I'll blaze ___ your fire, ___
while I'm ___ thirst - y?

then I'll sat - is - fy your,
Or would you cool me down

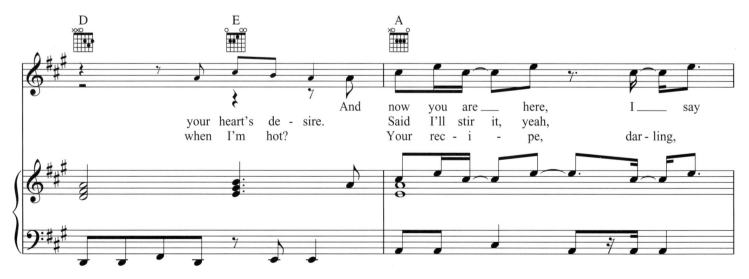

your heart's de - sire.
when I'm hot?

And now you are ___ here, I ___ say
Said I'll stir it, yeah,
Your rec - i - pe, dar - ling,

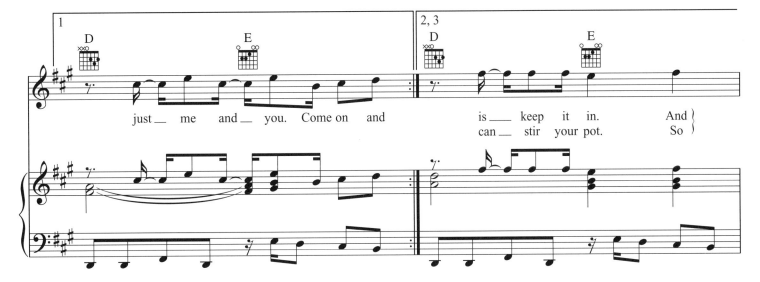

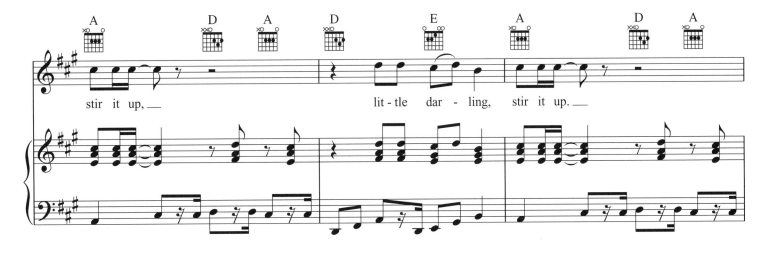

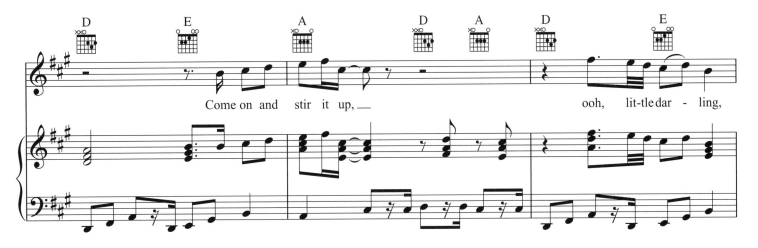

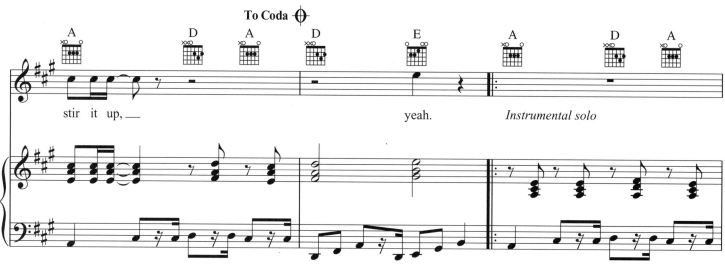

stir it up, ___   yeah.   *Instrumental solo*

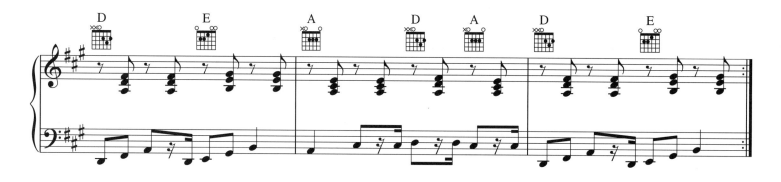

Solo ends

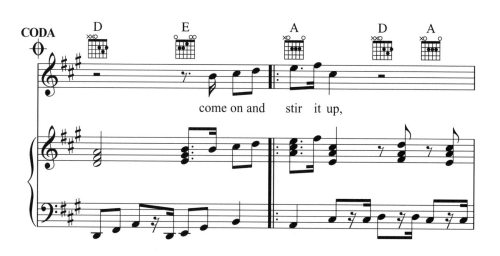

come on and   stir it up,

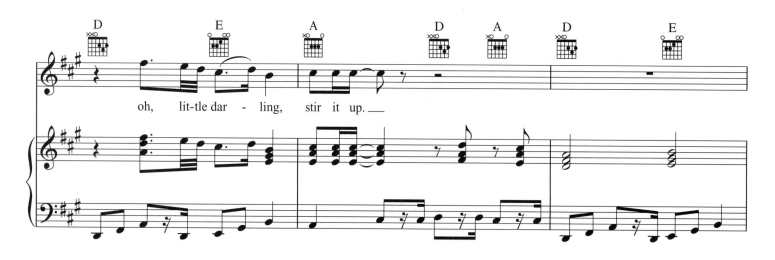

oh, lit-tle dar - ling,   stir it up. ___

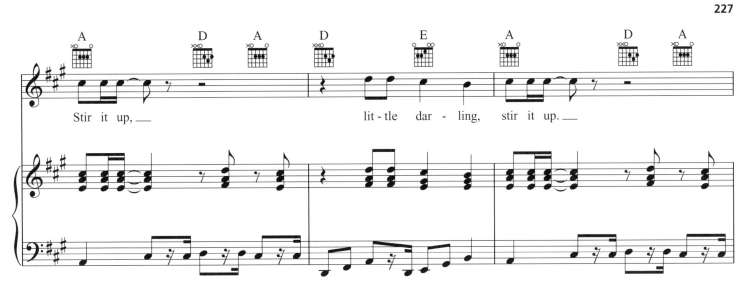

Stir it up, ___ lit - tle dar - ling, stir it up. ___

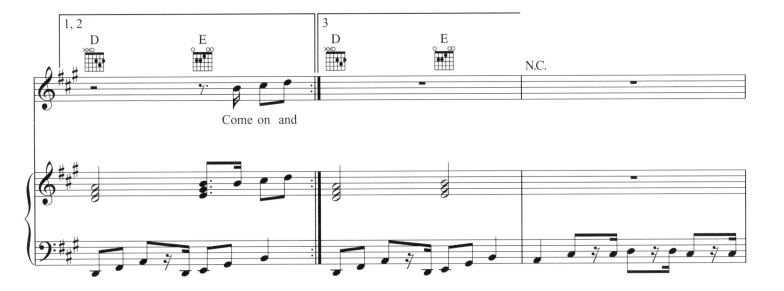

1, 2   3

Come on and

N.C.

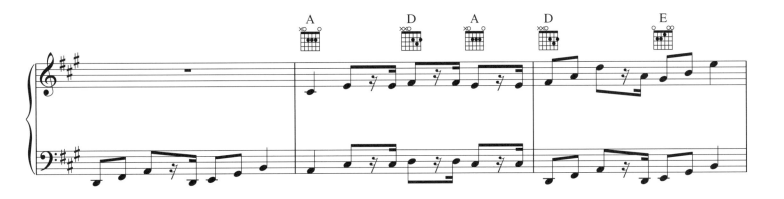

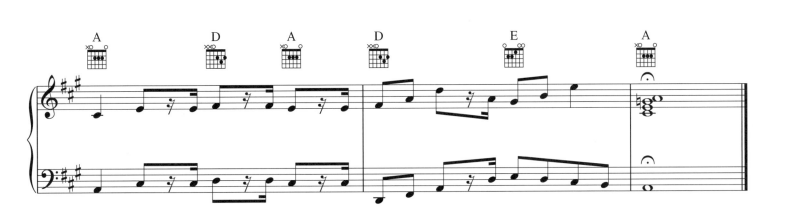

SUGAR, SUGAR

Words and Music by ANDY KIM
and JEFF BARRY

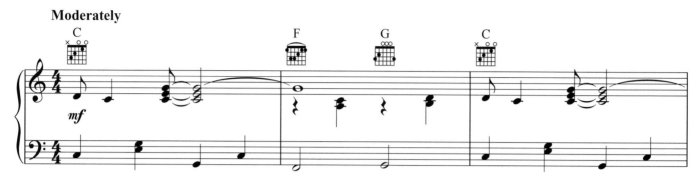

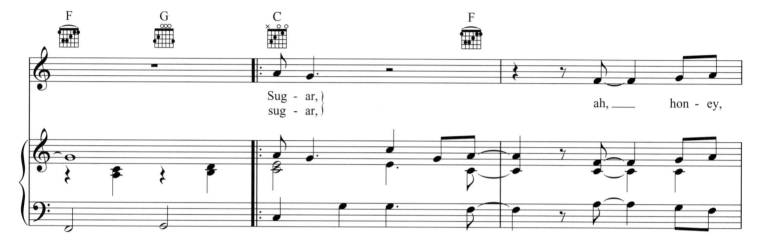

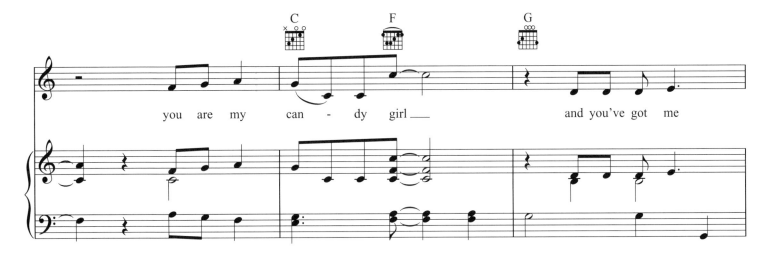

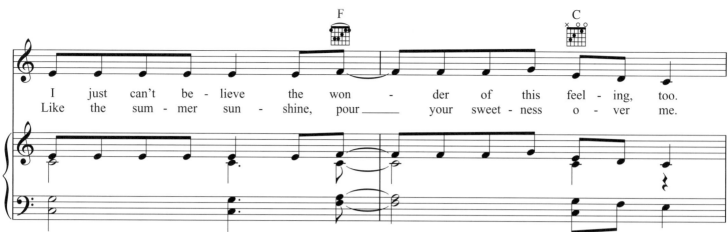

I just can't be- lieve the won- der of this feel- ing, too.
Like the sum- mer sun- shine, pour_____ your sweet- ness o- ver me.

1
(I just can't be- lieve it's true.)_____ Ah,

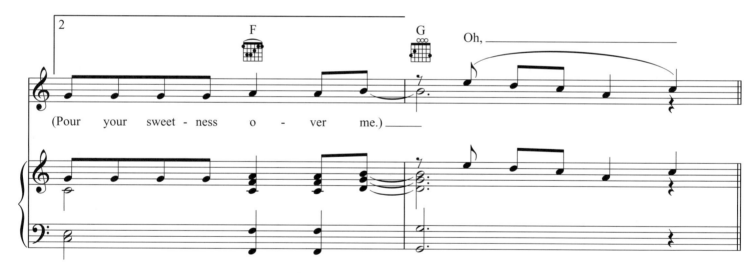

2
(Pour your sweet- ness o- ver me.)_____ Oh,_____

Pour a lit- tle sug- ar_____ on it, hon- ey.
Sug- ar,

Pour a lit - tle sug - ar ___ on it, ba - by.

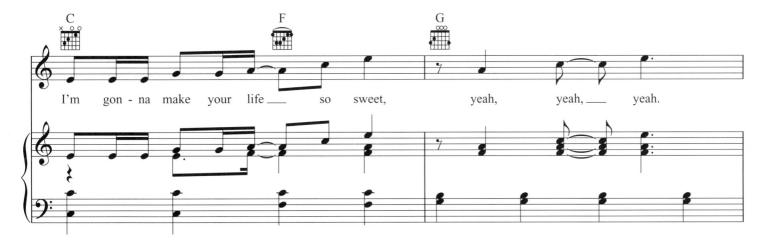

I'm gon - na make your life ___ so sweet, yeah, yeah, ___ yeah.

Pour a lit - tle ___ sug - ar on it, yeah, yeah, ___ yeah.

Pour a lit - tle sug - ar ___ on it, hon - ey. Ah!

SURFIN' U.S.A.

Words and Music by
CHUCK BERRY

bag - gies, _____ huar-a-chi san-dals, too. _____ A bush - y, bush - y blonde
sum - mer, _____ we're on sa-fa-ri to stay. _____ Tell the teach - er we're

hair - do, _____ surf - in' U. S. A. _____
surf - in', _____ surf - in' U. S. A. _____

___ You'll catch 'em surf - in' at Del Mar, _____ Ven - tu - ra Coun - ty Line, ___
___ At Hag - gar - ty's __ and Swam - i's, _____ Pa - cif - ic Pal - i - sades, _

_____ San - ta Cruz and Tres - sels, _____
_____ San O - no - fre and Sun - set, _____

THESE BOOTS ARE MADE FOR WALKIN'

Words and Music by
LEE HAZLEWOOD

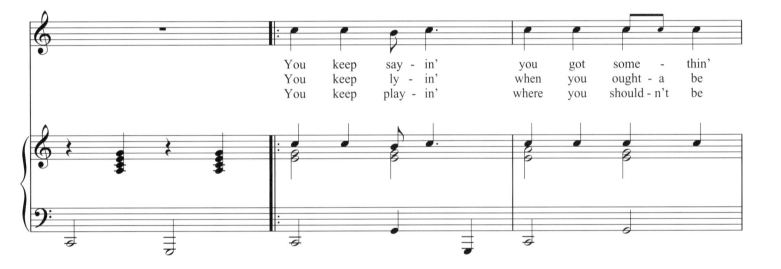

You keep say - in' you got some - thin'
You keep ly - in' when you ought - a be
You keep play - in' where you should - n't be

for me, some - thin' you call
"truth - in'," you keep los - in'
play - in', you keep think - in'

love but con - fess.
when you ought - a not bet.
that you'll nev - er get burned.

F

You been mess - in' where you should - n't been mess - in',
You keep "same - in'" when you ought - a be chang - in',
I just got me a brand - new box _____ of match - es,

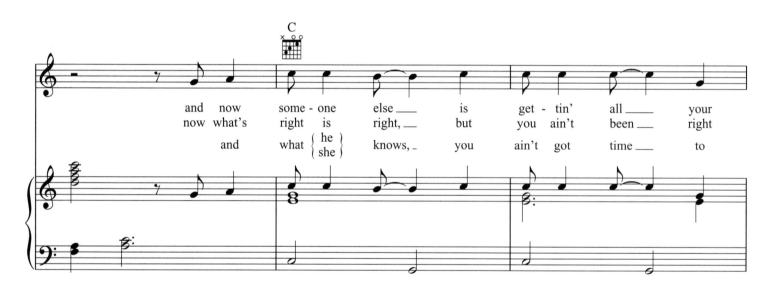

C

and now some - one else _____ is get - tin' all _____ your
now what's right is right, _____ but you ain't been _____ right
and what { he / she } knows, _ you ain't got time _____ to

C

best.
yet. }
learn. }

E♭

These boots are made _____ for

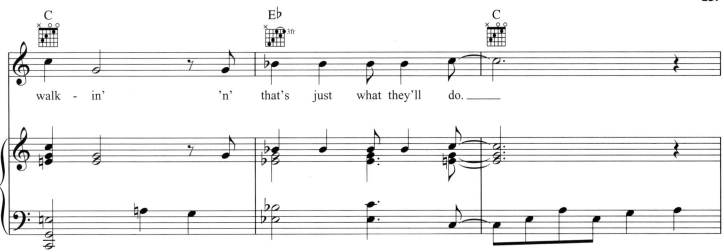

walk - in' 'n' that's just what they'll do. ____

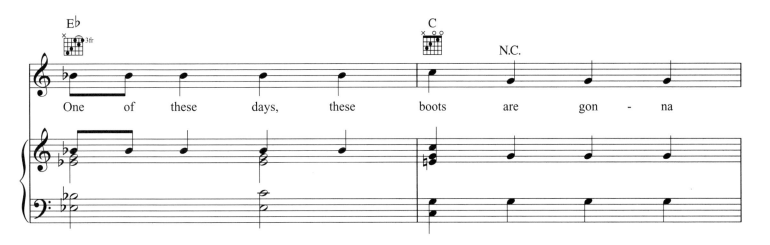

One of these days, these boots are gon - na

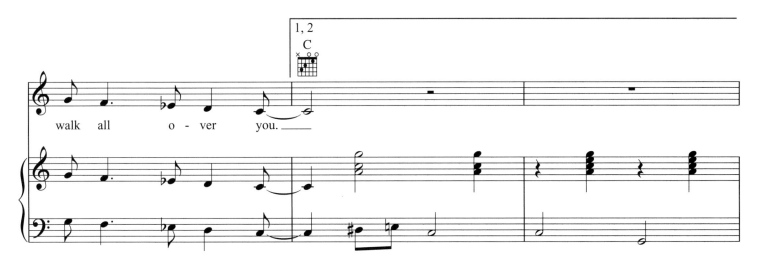

walk all o - ver you. ____

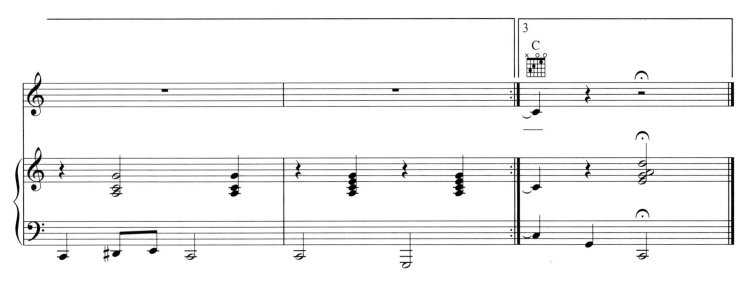

THIS LAND IS YOUR LAND

Words and Music by
WOODY GUTHRIE

Bright and cheerful

As I went

(1.) walk - ing _____ that rib - bon of high - way _____ I saw a -
(2.,4.,6.) your land, _____ this land is my land, _____ from Cal i -
(3.) ram - bled _____ and I fol-lowed my foot - steps _____ to the spar - kling
(5.) shin - ing, _____ and I was stroll - ing; the wheat fields

bove me _____ that end - less sky - way; _____ I saw be -
for - nia _____ to the New York is - land; _____ from the red - wood
sands of _____ her dia - mond des - erts; while all a -
wav - ing and the dust clouds roll - ing. _____ The fog was

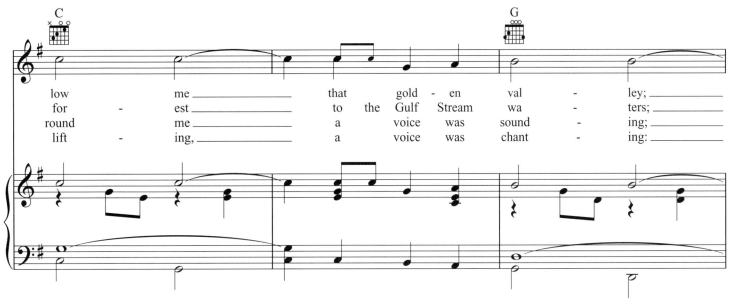

low me ____ that gold - en val - ley; ____
for - est ____ to the Gulf Stream wa - ters; ____
round me ____ a voice was sound - ing; ____
lift - ing, ____ a voice was chant - ing: ____

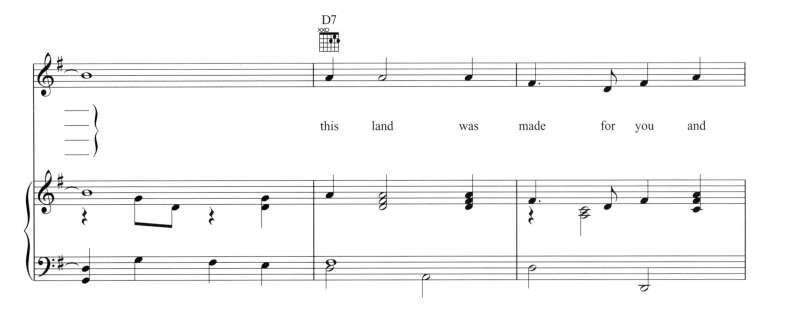

this land was made for you and

me. ____
(2.,4.,6. This land is
3. I've roamed and me. ____
5. Well, the sun came

rit.

TWIST AND SHOUT

Words and Music by BERT RUSSELL
and PHIL MEDLEY

Moderately, with a beat

Well, shake it up, ba - by, __ now,
- by, __ now, (Shake it up, ba - by) twist and
- by, __ now,

shout. ____ (Twist and shout) ____ Come on, come on, __ come on, ____ come on,

ba - by, _____ now,   Come on and work it on out. _____   (Work it on out)
(Come on, ba - by)

{ (1.) Well,   work   it   on   out, _____   (Work   it   on   out) __
{ (2., 3.) You know   you twist,   lit - tle   girl, _____   (Twist,   lit - tle   girl) __

_____ you know you look   so   good. __   (Look so   good) __ You know you got   me
_____ you know you twist   so   fine. __   (Twist so   fine) __ Come on and twist a   lit - tle

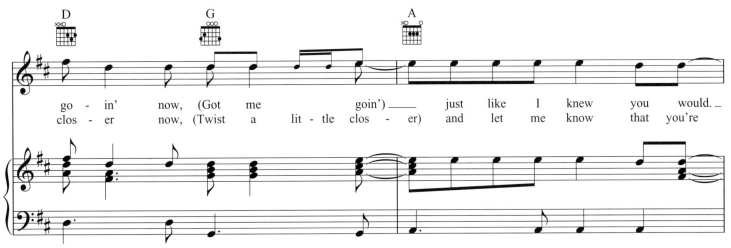

go - in'   now, (Got   me   goin') _____   just   like   I   knew   you   would. _
clos - er   now, (Twist a   lit - tle   clos - er)   and   let   me   know   that   you're

(Like I knew you would) ___ Well, shake it up, ba -
mine. (Let me know you're mine) _

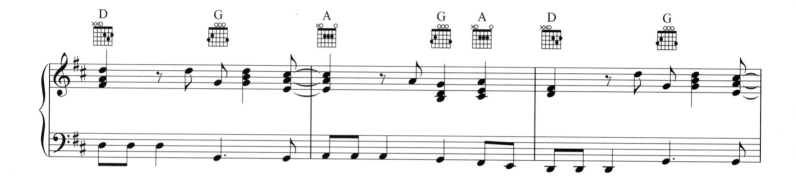

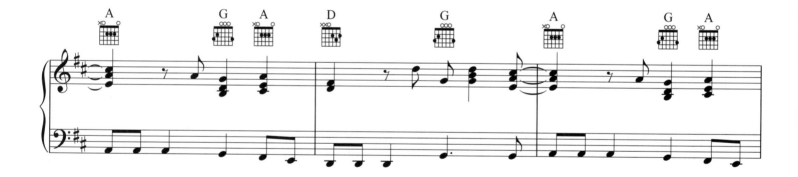

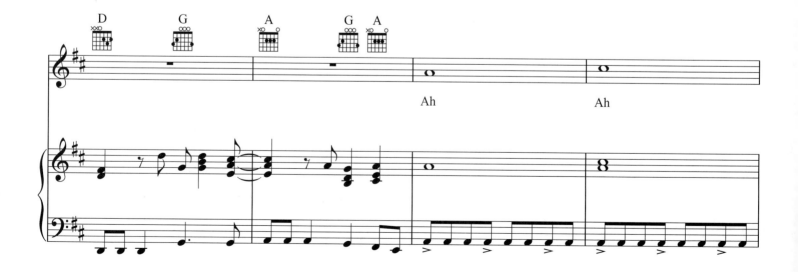

Ah   Ah

D.S. al Coda

Ah   Ah   Ah _____   Shake it up, ba-

CODA

___ Well, shake it, shake it, shake it, ba - by, now.
(Shake it up, ba-

Well, shake it, shake it, shake it, ba-by, now.
- by)   (Shake it up, ba - by.)   Ah

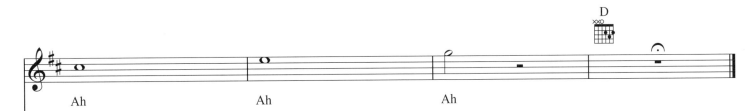

Ah   Ah   Ah

UP AROUND THE BEND

Words and Music by
JOHN FOGERTY

Moderately

There's a place _ up a - head, _ and I'm go - in' _ just as fast _ as my feet _

_ can fly. _ Come a - way, _ come a - way _ if you're go - in',

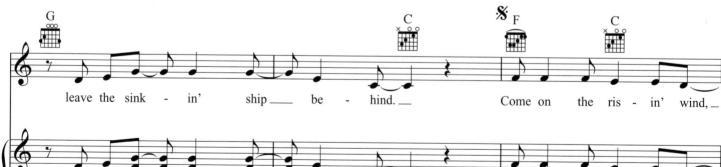

leave the sink - in' ship _ be - hind. _ Come on the ris - in' wind, _

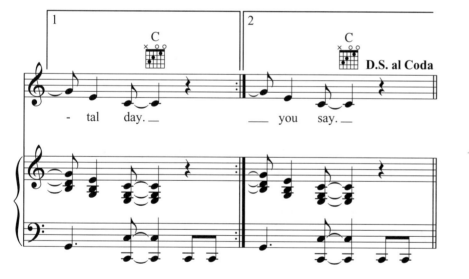

THREE LITTLE BIRDS

Words and Music by
BOB MARLEY

Moderately slow Reggae

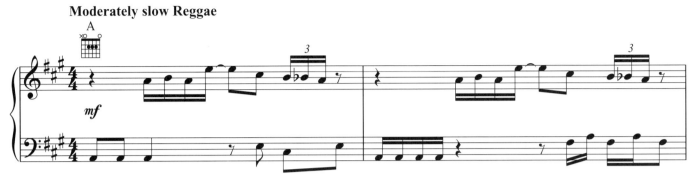

"Don't

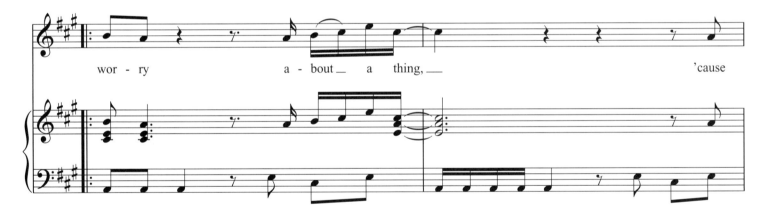

wor - ry   a - bout _ a   thing, _   'cause

ev - 'ry lit - tle thing   gon - na be al - right." _   Sing- in', "Don't

wor - ry a - bout _ a thing, _ 'cause

ev - 'ry lit - tle thing gon - na be al - right." _ Rise up this

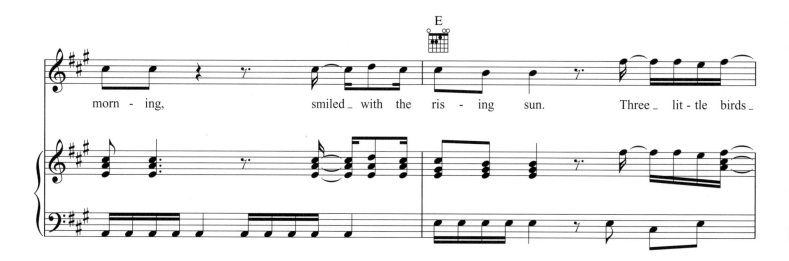

morn - ing, smiled _ with the ris - ing sun. Three _ lit - tle birds _

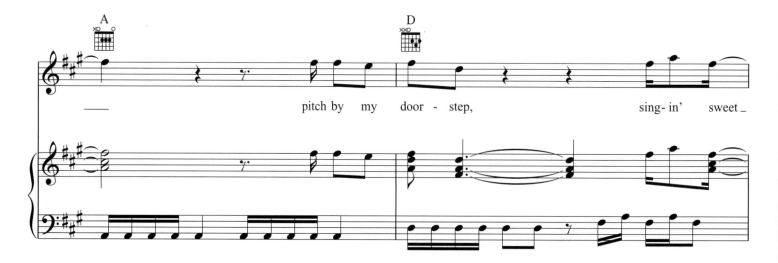

_ pitch by my door - step, sing- in' sweet _

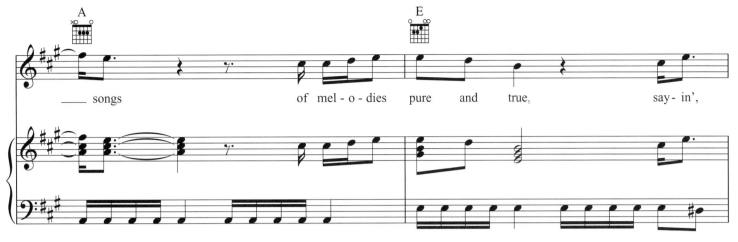

WALK OF LIFE

Words and Music by
MARK KNOPFLER

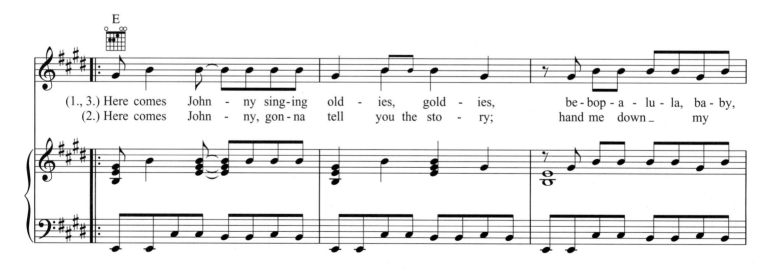

(1., 3.) Here comes John-ny sing-ing old-ies, gold-ies, be-bop-a-lu-la, ba-by,
(2.) Here comes John-ny, gon-na tell you the sto-ry; hand me down_ my

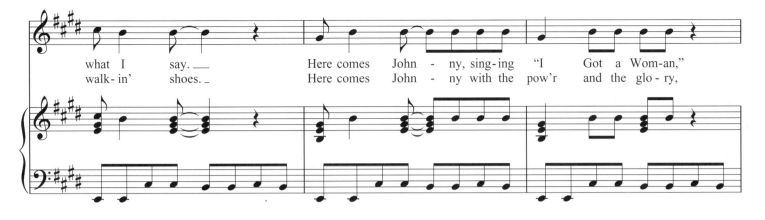

what I say. ___   Here comes John - ny, sing-ing "I   Got   a   Wom-an,"
walk-in'   shoes. _   Here comes John - ny with the pow'r   and the glo - ry,

down   in the tun-nel tryin' to   make   it   pay.   He got the ac - tion,
back - beat   the   talk - in'   blues. ___

A

he got the mo - tion.   Oh yeah, _   the   boy   can   play.

E

Ded - i - ca - tion, _   de - vo - tion,   turn - ing all the night - time

A   E

in - to the day. ___ { (1., 2.) He do the song a - bout the sweet lov - in'
(3.) And af - ter all the vio - lence and

B   E   A

wom - an,   he do the song a - bout the knife.   Then he do the
dou - ble - talk,   there's just a song in all the trou - ble and the strife.   You do the

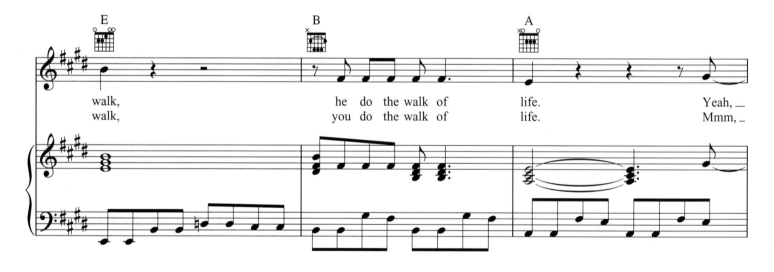

E   B   A

walk,   he do the walk of   life.   Yeah, __
walk,   you do the walk of   life.   Mmm, __

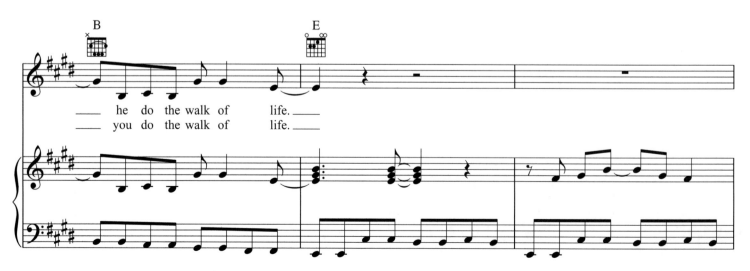

B   E

___ he do the walk of   life. ___
___ you do the walk of   life. ___

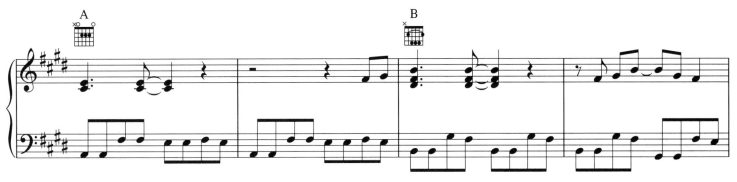

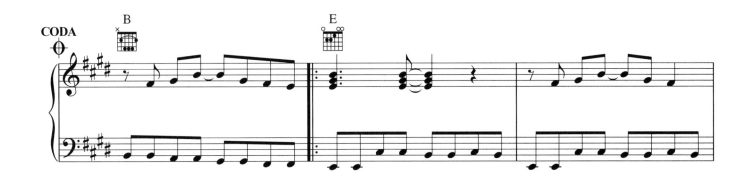

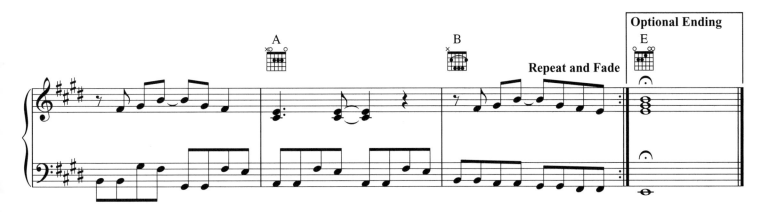

WORKING CLASS HERO

Words and Music by
JOHN LENNON

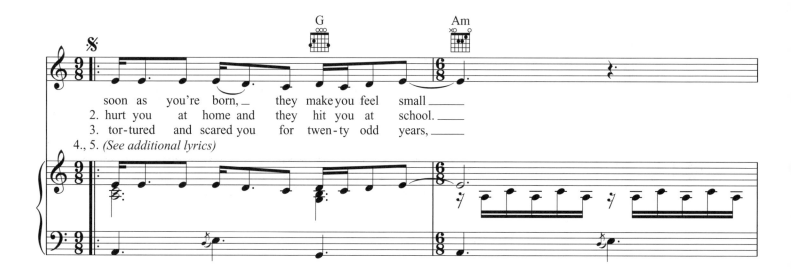

soon as you're born, ___ they make you feel small ___
2. hurt you at home and they hit you at school. ___
3. tor-tured and scared you for twen-ty odd years, ___
4., 5. *(See additional lyrics)*

by giv - ing you no time in-stead of it all, ___
They hate you if you're clev - er and they de-spise a fool, ___
then they ex - pect you to pick a ca - reer. ___

till the
till you're
when you

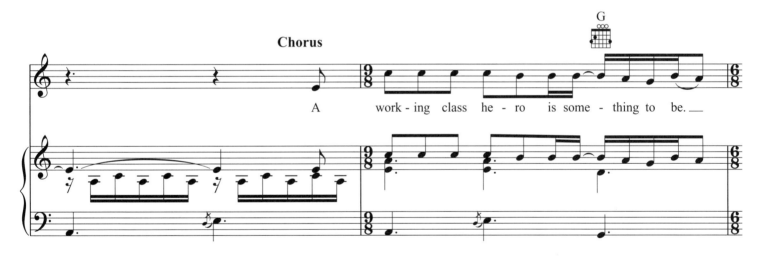

pain is so big you feel noth-ing at all. ___
so fuck-ing cra-zy you can't fol-low their rules.
can't real-ly func-tion, you're so full of fear. ___

Chorus

A work-ing class he - ro is some - thing to be. ___

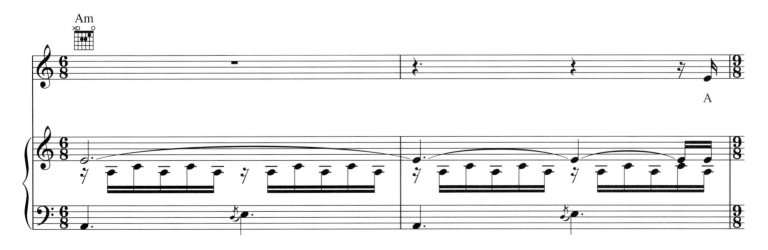

A

If you

want   to   be   a   he - ro,   well,   just   fol - low   me. __

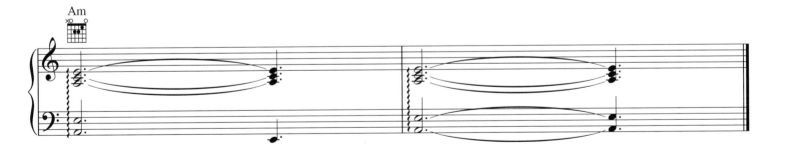

Additional Lyrics

4. Keep you doped with religion and sex and TV.
   And you think you're so clever and classless and free.
   But you're still fucking peasants as far as I can see.
   Chorus

5. There's room at the top they are telling you still.
   But first you must learn how to smile as you kill
   If you want to be like the folks on the hill.
   Chorus

WEREWOLVES OF LONDON

Words and Music by WARREN ZEVON,
WADDY WACHTEL and LEROY MARINELL

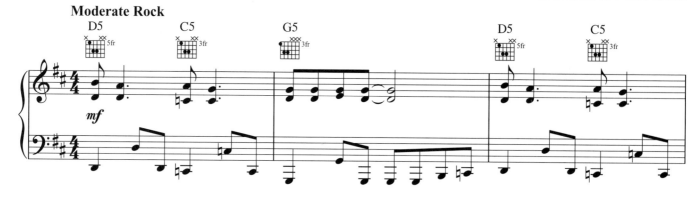

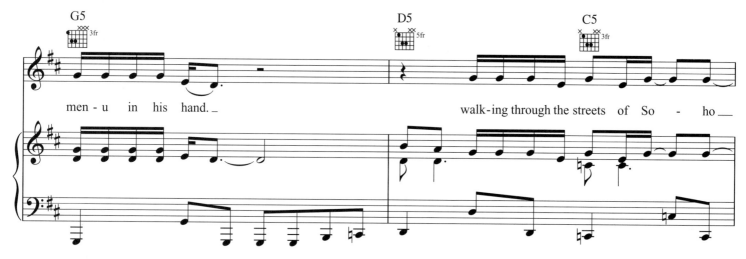

Ow - ooh! _____ Well, I saw Lon Cha - ney walk-

- ing with the Queen, _ do - in' the were - wolves of Lon - don. _

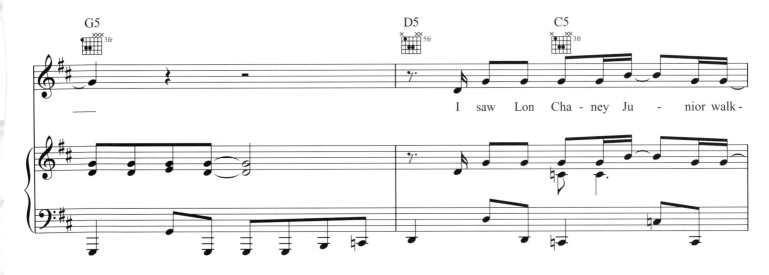

_ I saw Lon Cha - ney Ju - nior walk-

- ing with the Queen, _ do - in' the were - wolves of Lon - don. _